SILVER·BURDETT

Making Music

Resource Book

Teacher's Edition Part Three
Kindergarten

PEARSON

Scott
Foresman

Editorial Offices: Glenview, Illinois • Parsippany, New Jersey • New York, New York
Sales Offices: Needham, Massachusetts • Duluth, Georgia • Glenview, Illinois
Coppell, Texas • Sacramento, California • Mesa, Arizona

ISBN: 0-382-36622-0

Copyright © 2005, Pearson Education, Inc.

Program Authors

Jane Beethoven

Susan Brumfield

Patricia Shehan Campbell

David N. Connors

Robert A. Duke

Judith A. Jellison

Rita Klinger

Rochelle Mann

Hunter C. March

Nan L. McDonald

Marvelene C. Moore

Mary Palmer

Konnie Saliba

Will Schmid

Carol Scott-Kassner

Mary E. Shamrock

Sandra L. Stauffer

Judith Thomas

Jill Trinka

Resource Book Contributing Authors

Jane Beethoven	Activity Masters
Susan Brumfield	Music Reading Worksheets Music Reading Practice
David N. Connors	Orff
Alice-Ann Darrow	Signing
Robert A. Duke	Assessment
Martha F. Hilley	Keyboard
Debbie Burgoon Hines	Pronunciation Practice Guides
Judith A. Jellison	Assessment
Rita Klinger	Music Reading Worksheets Music Reading Practice
Shirley Lacroix	Recorder
Rochelle Mann	Music Reading Worksheets Music Reading Practice
Konnie Saliba	Orff
Julie K. Scott	Orff Recorder
Judith Thomas	Orff
Jill Trinka	Music Reading Worksheets Music Reading Practice
CP Language Institute	Pronunciation Practice Guides

Master Table of Contents

PRONUNCIATION PRACTICE GUIDE

Recorded Pronunciation Practice tracks are provided in the CD package.

Table of Contents

PRONUNCIATION PRACTICE 1

O ma washi
(Go Around the Cat's Eye)

Folk Song from Japan

Phrase ① *O ma wa-shi, O ma wa-shi,*
   oh mah wah-shee, oh mah wah-shee,

② *Ne ko-no-me*
   neh koh-noh-meh.

PRONUNCIATION PRACTICE 2

Ikhanda, maslombe (My Head and My Shoulders)

Zulu Children's Game Song

Phrase ① *I-kha-nda,*
ee-kah-ndah,

② *ma-slo-mbe,*
mah-shyoh-mbeh,

③ *si-fu-ba, no-kha-lo,*
see-foo-bah, noh-kah-loh,

④ *'ma-do-lo, 'na-ma-zwa-ne,*
mah-doh-loh, nah-mah-zwah-neh,

⑤ *'ma-do-lo, 'na-ma-zwa-ne.*
mah-doh-loh, nah-mah-zwah-neh.

Pronunciation Practice 3

Los trencitos (Little Trains)

Folk Song from Venezuela

Phrase ① *Los tren-ci-tos van*
lohs trehn-see-tohs vahn

② *y vie-nen re-so-plan-do*
ee vyeh-nehn reh-soh-plahn-doh

③ *sin ce-sar.*
seen seh-sahr.

④ *Par-ten, co-rren,*
pahr-tehn, koh-rrehn,

⑤ *se de-tie-nen,*
seh deh-tyeh-nehn,

⑥ *lue-go, vuel-ven*
lweh-goh, vwehl-vehn

⑦ *a em-pe-zar.*
ah‿ehm-peh-sahr.

Kindergarten, Teacher Edition, page 24

PRONUNCIATION PRACTICE 4

Mbombera

Folk Song from Zimbabwe

Phrase ① *Mbom-be-ra,*
mbahm-beh-rah,

② *Mbom-be-ra*
mbahm-beh-rah

③ *ye sti-me-la.*
yeh stee-meh-lah.

④ *Na-na na na na,*
nah-nah nah nah nah,

⑤ *Na-na na na na,*
nah-nah nah nah nah,

⑥ *Na-na na na na,*
nah-nah nah nah nah,

⑦ *Na-na na na na.*
nah-nah nah nah nah.

Pronunciation Practice 5

Kuma san (Little Bear)

Children's Rope Skipping Song from the Sendai District, Japan

Phrase ① *Ku-ma san, Ku-ma san,*
koo-mah sahn, koo-mah sahn,

② *Ma-wa-re-mi-gi.*
mah-wah-reh-mee-ghee.

③ *Ku-ma san, Ku-ma san,*
koo-mah sahn, koo-mah sahn,

④ *Ryo te wo tsui te*
ryoh teh oh tsoo-ee teh

⑤ *Ku-ma san, Ku-ma san,*
koo-mah sahn, koo-mah sahn,

⑥ *Ka-ta a-shi a-ge te,*
kah-tah ah-shee ah-geh teh,

⑦ *Ku-ma san, Ku-ma san,*
koo-mah sahn, koo-mah sahn,

⑧ *"Sa-yo-na-ra."*
"sah-yoh-nah-rah."

© Pearson Education, Inc.

PRONUNCIATION PRACTICE 6

Pon, pon, pon (Tap, Tap, Tap)

Children's Game from Mexico

Verse 1

Phrase ① *Pon, pon, pon.*
pohn, pohn, pohn.

② *Pon, pon-y-pon.*
pohn, pohn-ee-pohn.

③ *Pon el de-di-to*
pohn ehl deh-dee-toh

④ *En la ma-ni-ta.*
ehn lah mah-nee-tah.

Verse 2

Phrase ① *Pon, pon, pon.*
pohn, pohn, pohn.

② *Pon, pon-y-pon.*
pohn, pohn-ee-pohn.

③ *Pon el de-di-to*
pohn ehl deh-dee-toh

④ *En la ca-ri-ta.*
ehn lah kah-rree-tah.

Verse 3

Phrase ① *Pon, pon, pon.*
pohn, pohn, pohn.

② *Pon, pon-y-pon.*
pohn, pohn-ee-pohn.

③ *Pon el de-di-to*
pohn ehl deh-dee-toh

④ *En la na-ri-ci-ta.*
ehn lah nah-ree-see-tah.

Verse 4

Phrase ① *Pon, pon, pon.*
pohn, pohn, pohn.

② *Pon, pon-y-pon.*
pohn, pohn-ee-pohn.

③ *Pon el de-di-to*
pohn ehl deh-dee-toh

④ *En los o-ji-tos.*
ehn lohs oh-hee-tohs.

Pronunciation Practice 7

¡Qué llueva! (It's Raining!)

Folk Song from Puerto Rico

Phrase ① *¡Qué llue-va! ¡Qué llue-va!*
keh chweh-vah! keh chweh-vah!

② *la vir-gen de la cue-va,*
lah veer-hehn deh lah kweh-vah,

③ *los pa-ja-ri-tos can-tan*
lohs pah-hah-ree-tohs kahn-tahn

④ *las nu-bes se le-van-tan.*
lahs noo-behs seh leh-vahn-thahn.

⑤ *¡Qué si! ¡Qué no!*
keh see! keh noh!

⑥ *¡Qué cai-ga̤el cha-pa-rrón!*
keh kahee-gah̤ehl chah-pah-rrohn!

Kindergarten, Teacher Edition, page 81

PRONUNCIATION PRACTICE 8

Luna lunera (Moon, Moonlight)   *Children's Playground Rhyme from Cuba*

Phrase ① *Lu-na lu-ne-ra,*
loo-nah loo-neh-rah,

② *cas-ca-be-le-ra,*
kahs-kah-beh-leh-rah,

③ *cin-co to-ri-tos*
seen-koh toh-ree-tohs

④ *y‿u-na ter-ne-ra.*
ee‿oo-nah tehr-neh-rah.

Mon son pha
(Mon Hides the Cloth)

Mon Rhyme from Western Thailand

Verse 1

Phrase ① *Mon son pha*
mohn sohn pah

② *tuk-ka-ta yu kang lung*
took-kah-tah yoo hkuhng luhng

③ *wai non wai ni*
wah_ee nohn wah_ee nee

④ *chan cha ti kon thoe*
chuhn chuh tee kohn tuh_uh

© PEARSON EDUCATION, INC.

Kindergarten, Teacher Edition, page 91

PRONUNCIATION PRACTICE 10

Ég a gyertya
(Candle Burning Bright)

Children's Song from Hungary

Verse 1

Phrase ① *Ég a gyer-tya ég,*
ehg uh dyehr-tyah ehg,

② *el ne a-lud-jék,*
ehl neh ah-loo-dyeek,

③ *A-ki lán-got*
uh-kee lahn-goht

④ *lát-ni a-kar*
laht-nee ah-kahr

⑤ *mind le-gug-gel-jék.*
meend leh-goo-guhl-yeek.

© PEARSON EDUCATION, INC.

Mi cuerpo hace música (There's Music in Me)

Folk Song from Puerto Rico

Refrain

Phrase ① *Mi cuer-po, mi cuer-po*
mee kwehr-poh, mee kwehr-poh

② *ha-ce mú-si-ca.*
ah-seh moo-see-kah.

③ *Mi cuer-po, mi cuer-po*
mee kwehr-poh, mee kwehr-poh

④ *ha-ce mú-si-ca.*
ah-seh moo-see-kah.

Verse 1

Phrase ① *Mi bo-ca ha-ce la, la, la.*
mee boh-kah ah-seh lah, lah, lah.

② *Mis ma-nos ha-cen (clap, clap, clap)*
mees mah-nohs ah-sehn

③ *Mis pies ha-cen ta, ta, ta.*
mees pee‿ehs ah-sehn tah, tah, tah.

④ *Mi cin-tu-ra ha-ce Cha, cha, cha.*
mee sehn-too-rah ah-seh chah, chah, chah.

⑤ *Cha, cha, cha. Mi cin-tu-ra ha-ce cha, cha, cha.*
chah, chah, chah. mee sehn-too-rah ah-seh chah, chah, chah.

⑥ *Cha, cha, cha. Mi cin-tu-ra ha-ce cha, cha, cha.*
chah, chah, chah. mee sehn-too-rah ah-seh chah, chah, chah.

PRONUNCIATION PRACTICE 12

Kunolounkwa

Oneida Lullaby Adapted by Joanne Shenandoah

Phrase ① *Sun-dow sun-dow oh-we-las*
Suhn-dow suhn-dow oh-wheh-lahs

② *ku-no-lo-un-kwa.*
goo-noh-loh-oon-kwah.

③ *Ne' tsi so' tsi,*
Neh dzee soh dzee,

④ *sik sat dee,*
sihk saht dee,

⑤ *ku-no-lo-un-kwa.*
goo-noh-loh-oon-kwah.

Vamos a hacer la ronda (Let's Make a Circle)

Spanish Words and Music by María Alvarez Ríos

Refrain

Phrase ① *Va-mos a_ha-cer la ron-da,*
vah-mohs ah-sehr lah rohn-dah,

② *den-se las ma-nos ya.*
dehn-seh lahs mah-nohs dyah.

③ *Den-se las ma-nos to-dos*
dehn-seh lahs mah-nohs toh-dohs

④ *va-mos a sal-tar.*
vah-mohs ah sahl-tahrr.

Verse 1

Phrase ① *A sal-tar, a sal-tar,*
ah sahl-tahrr, ah sahl-tahrr,

② *va-mos a sal-tar.*
vah-mohs ah sahl-tahrr.

③ *A sal-tar, a sal-tar,*
ah sahl-tahrr, ah sahl-tahrr,

④ *va-mos a sal-tar.*
vah-mohs ah sahl-tahrr.

Verse 2

Phrase ① *Des-can-sar, des-can-sar,*
dehs-kahn-sahrr, dehs-kahn-sahrr,

② *va-mos a des-can-sar.*
vah-mohs ah dehs-kahn-sahrr.

PRONUNCIATION PRACTICE 13 (CONTINUED)

③ *Des-can-sar, des-can-sar,*
dehs-kahn-sahrr, dehs-kahn-sahrr,

④ *va-mos a des-can-sar.*
vah-mohs ah dehs-kahn-sahrr.

Verse 3

Phrase ① *Ca-mi-nar, ca-mi-nar,*
kah-mee-nahrr, kah-mee-nahrr,

② *va-mos a ca-mi-nar.*
vah-mohs ah kah-mee-nahrr.

③ *Ca-mi-nar, ca-mi-nar,*
kah-mee-nahrr, kah-mee-nahrr,

④ *va-mos a ca-mi-nar.*
vah-mohs ah kah-mee-nahrr.

Verse 4

Phrase ① *A co-rrer, a co-rrer,*
ah koh-rrehrr, ah koh-rrehrr,

② *va-mos a co-rrer.*
vah-mohs ah koh-rrehrr.

③ *A co-rrer, a co-rrer,*
ah koh-rrehrr, ah koh-rrehrr,

④ *va-mos a co-rrer.*
vah-mohs ah koh-rrehrr.

Verse 5

Phrase ① *Sa-lu-dar, sa-lu-dar,*
sah-loo-dahrr, sah-loo-dahrr,

② *va-mos a sa-lu-dar.*
vah-mohs ah sah-loo-dahrr.

③ *Sa-lu-dar, sa-lu-dar,*
sah-loo-dahrr, sah-loo-dahrr,

④ *va-mos a sa-lu-dar.*
vah-mohs ah sah-loo-dahrr.

PRONUNCIATION PRACTICE 14

El caracol (The Snail's Dance)

Children's Song from Spain

Verse 1

Phrase ① *Ca-ra-col, col, col,*
kah-rah-kohl, kohl, kohl,

② *sal de tu ca-si-ta,*
sahl deh too kah-see-tah,

③ *Que‿es de ma-ña-ni-ta*
keh‿ehs deh mah-nyah-nee-tah

④ *y‿ha sal-li-do‿el sol.*
ee‿yah sah-lee-doh‿ehl sohl.

Verse 2

Phrase ① *Ca-ra-col, col, col,*
kah-rah-kohl, kohl, kohl,

② *vuel-va‿a tu ca-si-ta,*
vwehl-veh‿ah too kah-see-tah,

③ *Que‿es de no-che-ci-ta*
keh‿ehs deh noh-cheh-see-tah

④ *y se‿ha pue-sto‿el sol.*
ee seh‿ah pwehs-toh‿ehl sohl.

Ee jer ha ba go (The Hungry Dog)

Children's Song from China

Phrase ① *Ee jer ha ba go*
ee jeer hah bah goh

② *Tzwoa tsai da-men ko;*
dzwoh dsahee dah-mehn koh;

③ *Yen jing hey yo yo*
yehn jeeng heh yoh yoh

④ *Shiang cher lao qu toe.*
shee‿ahng chuhr lah‿oo goo toh.

Kindergarten, Teacher Edition, page 133

PRONUNCIATION PRACTICE 16

Bereleh (Little Snail)

Children's Song from Israel
Collected in Jerusalem by Rita Klinger

Phrase ① *Be-re-leh, Be-re-leh,*
beh-rah-leh, beh-rah-leh,

② *tse a-chu-tsa*
tseh hah-hkhoo-tsah

③ *A-ba v'e i-ma-*
ah-bah veh-ee-muh-

④ *y' knu l'e cha u-ga.*
eek-noo leh hkhah oo-gah.

Koriko!

*Children's Marching Song from
Senegal, West Africa*

Phrase ① *Koriko!*
kuh-ree-koh!

② *Ko-ri ko-ri ko.*
kuh-ree kuh-ree kuh.

③ *Koriko!*
kuh-ree-koh!

④ *Ko-ri ko-ri ko.*
kuh-ree kuh-ree kuh.

⑤ *Ay, yam-ba-la,*
ah‿ee yuhm-bah-lah,

⑥ *yam-ba-la ma-ma.*
yuhm-bah-lah mah-mah.

⑦ *Ay, yam-ba-la,*
ah‿ee yuhm-bah-lah,

⑧ *yam-ba-la ma-ma.*
yuhm-bah-lah mah-mah.

Kindergarten, Teacher Edition, page 154

PRONUNCIATION PRACTICE 18

Fais dodo (Close Your Eyes)

Folk Song from France

Phrase ① *Fais do-do,*
feh doh-doh,

② *'co-las, mon p'tit frère*
koh-lah mo(n) p'tee freh-ruh

③ *Fais do-do,*
feh doh-doh,

④ *T'au ras du lo-lo,*
toh rah dew loh-loh,

⑤ *Pa-pa est en bas,*
pah-pah eh taw(n) bah,

⑥ *il fait du choc'-lat.*
ihl feh dew shohw-klah.

⑦ *Ma-man est en haut,*
mah-moh eh taw(n) oh,

⑧ *elle fait du ga-teau.*
ehl feh dew gah-toh.

Yang wa wa (Nursery Song)

Children's Song from Taiwan

Phrase ① *Yang wa wa*
yuhng wah wah

② *Xiao xi xi*
shyow shee shee

③ *Yu le yi ge*
yah‿ow luh ee guh

④ *Yang wa wa.*
yuhng wah wah.

⑤ *Ni‿tsung na li lai,*
nee‿tsuhng nah lee lah‿ee,

⑥ *Ni‿wang na li chu,*
nee‿wuhng nah lee choo,

⑦ *Yu le yi ge*
yah‿ow luh ee guh

⑧ *Yang wa wa.*
yuhng wah wah.

PRONUNCIATION PRACTICE 20

Los pollitos (Baby Chicks)

Folk Song from Puerto Rico

Verse 1

Phrase ① *Los po-lli-tos di-cen:*
lohs poh-djee-tohs dee-sehn:

② *"Pí-o, pí-o, pí-o,"*
pee-oh, pee-oh, pee-oh,

③ *Cuan-do tie-nen ham-bre,*
kwahn-doh tee‿eh-nehn ahm-breh,

④ *Cuan-do tie-nen frí-o.*
kwahn-doh tee‿eh-nehn free-oh.

Verse 2

Phrase ① *La ga-lli-na bus-ca*
lah gah-djee-nah boos-kah

② *El ma-íz el tri-go,*
ehl mah-ees ehl tree-goh,

③ *Les da la co-mi-da*
lehs dah lah koh-mee-dah

④ *Y les pre-sta‿a-bri-go.*
ee lehs preh-stah‿ah-bree-goh.

Verse 3

Phrase ① *Ba-jo sus dos a-las*
bah-hoh soos dohs ah-lahs

② *A-cu-rru-ca-di-tos*
ah-koo-rroo-kah-dee-tohs

③ *Ha-sta‿el o-tro dí-a*
ah-stah‿ehl oh-troh dee-ah

④ *Duer-men los po-lli-tos.*
dwehr-mehn lohs poh-djee-tohs.

A la rurru niño
(Hush, My Little Baby)

Folk Song from Mexico

Phrase ① *A la ru-rru ni-ño,*
ah lah rroo-rroo nee-nyoh,

② *A la ru-rru ya,*
ah lah rroo-rroo yah,

③ *Duér-me-te, mi ni-ño,*
dwehrr-meh-teh, mee nee-nyoh,

④ *Y duér-me-te ya.*
ee dwehr-meh-teh yah.

PRONUNCIATION PRACTICE 22

Kaeru no uta (The Frog Song)

Children's Song from Japan

Phrase ① *Ka-e-ru no u-ta ga*
kah-eh-roo noh oo-tah gah

② *Ki-ko-e-te ku-ru-yo*
kee-koh-eh-teh koo-roo-yoh

③ *Gwa! Gwa! Gwa! Gwa!*
gwah! gwah! gwah! gwah!

④ *Ge-ro, ge-ro, ge-ro, ge-ro,*
geh-roh, geh-roh, geh-roh, geh-roh,

⑤ *gwa, gwa, gwa!*
gwah, gwah, gwah!

PRONUNCIATION PRACTICE 23

¿Dónde lo escondí? (Where Did I Hide It?)

Spanish Words and Music by María Alvarez Ríos

Phrase ① *¿Dón-de lo_es-con-dí? A-quí.*
dohn-deh loh_ehs-kohn-dee? ah-kee.

② *¿Dón-de lo_es-con-dí? A-cá.*
dohn-deh loh_ehs-kohn-dee? ah-kah.

③ *¿Y_ah-o-ra dón-de_es-tá? A-quí.*
ee_ah-oh-rah dohn-deh_ehs-tah? ah-kee.

④ *¿Y_ah-o-ra dón-de_es-tá? A-cá.*
ee_ah-oh-rah dohn-deh_ehs-tah? ah-kah.

PRONUNCIATION PRACTICE 24

Juan pirulero (John Lollypop-Seller)

Children's Song from Mexico

Phrase ① *Es-te es_el jue-go*
ehs-teh ehs_ehl wheh-goh

② *de Juan pi-ru-le-ro.*
deh whahn pee-roo-leh-roh.

③ *Que ca-da*
keh kah-dah

④ *quien a-tien-de*
kyehn ah-tyehn-deh

⑤ *a su jue-go.*
ah soo wheh-goh.

PRONUNCIATION PRACTICE 25

Les petites marionettes
(The Little Marionettes)

Children's Song from France

Phrase ① *Ain-si font, font, font,*
uhn-see foh(n), foh(n), foh(n),

② *Les pe-ti-tes ma-rio-net-tes;*
leh puh-tee-tuh mah-ree‿yuh-neh-tuh;

③ *Ain-si font, font, font,*
uhn-see foh(n), foh(n), foh(n),

④ *Trois p'tits tour*
twah ptee toor

⑤ *et puis s'en vont.*
eh pwee sawn voh(n).

Perná, perná, i mélissá
(Fly By, Fly By)

Children's Game from Greece
From the Collection of Danai Gagné

Phrase ① *Per-ná, per-ná i mé-lis-sá*
per-nah, per-nah ee meh-lee-sah

② *méh ta mé-lis-só-pou-lá*
meh tah meh-lee-soh-poo-lah

③ *keh mah tá peh-thó-pou-lá.*
keh mah thah peh-thhoh-poo-lah.

PRONUNCIATION PRACTICE 27

Sh'ney dubim (Two Bears)

Words and Music by
Judith Eisenstein and Frieda Prensky

Phrase ① *Dov! Dov! Sh'ney du-bim*
dohv! dohv! shneh doo-bihm

② *mit-gal-ge-lim,*
miht-gahl-geh-lihm,

③ *mit-gal-ge-lim,*
miht-gahl-geh-lihm,

④ *mit-gal-ge-lim*
miht-gahl-geh-lihm

⑤ *sh'ney du-bim,*
shneh doo-bihm,

⑥ *sh'ney du-bim hu-mim.*
shneh doo-bihm hoo-mihm.

El burrito enfermo
(The Sick Little Donkey)

Children's Song from Spain

Verse 1

Phrase ① *A mi bu-rro, a mi bu-rro*
ah mee boo-rroh, ah mee boo-rroh

② *le due-le la ca-be-za,*
leh dweh-leh lah kah-beh-sah,

③ *y el mé-di-co le man-da*
ee yehl meh-dee-koh leh mahn-dah

④ *u-na go-rri-ta ne-gra,*
oo-nah goh-rree-tah neh-grah,

⑤ *u-na go-rri-ta ne-gra*
oo-nah goh-rree-tah neh-grah

⑥ *y que mue-va las pa-ti-tas*
ee keh mweh-vah lahs pah-tee-tahs

⑦ *tap, tap, tap, tap.*
tahp, tahp, tahp, tahp.

Verse 2

Phrase ① *A mi bu-rro, a mi bu-rro*
ah mee boo-rroh, ah mee boo-rroh

② *le due-le la gar-gan-ta,*
leh dweh-leh lah gahr-gahn-tah,

③ *y el mé-di-co le man-da*
ee yehl meh-dee-koh leh mahn-dah

PRONUNCIATION PRACTICE 28 (CONTINUED)

④ *u-na bu-fan-da blan-ca,*
oo-nah boo-fahn-dah blahn-kah,

⑤ *u-na bu-fan-da blan-ca*
oo-nah boo-fahn-dah blahn-kah

⑥ *y que mue-va las pa-ti-tas*
ee keh mweh-vah lahs pah-tee-tahs

⑦ *tap, tap, tap, tap.*
tahp, tahp, tahp, tahp.

Verse 3

Phrase ① *A mi bu-rro, a mi bu-rro*
ah mee boo-rroh, ah mee boo-rroh

② *le due-len las o-re-jas,*
leh dweh-lehn lahs oh-reh-hahs,

③ *y el mé-di-co le man-da*
ee yehl meh-dee-koh leh mahn-dah

④ *u-nas o-re-je-ras ro-jas,*
oo-nahs oh-reh heh-rahs roh-hahs,

⑤ *u-nas o-re-je-ras ro-jas*
oo-nahs oh-reh heh-rahs roh-hahs

⑥ *y que mue-va las pa-ti-tas*
ee keh mweh-vah lahs pah-tee-tahs

⑦ *tap, tap, tap, tap.*
tahp, tahp, tahp, tahp.

Vamos a cantar (Let's Sing!)

Words and Music by José-Luis Orozco

Verse 1

Phrase ① *A̶ho-ra va-ya a can-tar,*
ah‿oh-rah bah-yah ah kahn-tahrr,

② *a can-tar, a can-tar.*
ah kahn-tahrr, ah kahn-tahrr.

③ *A̶ho-ra va-mos a can-tar,*
ah‿oh-rah bah-mohs ah kahn-tahrr,

④ *a can-tar, a can-tar.*
ah kahn-tahrr, ah kahn-tahrr.

Verse 2

Phrase ① *A̶ho-ra va-ya a le-er,*
ah‿oh-rah bah-yah ah leh-ehrr,

② *a le-er, a le-er.*
ah leh-ehrr, ah leh-ehrr.

③ *A̶ho-ra va-mos a le-er,*
ah‿oh-rah bah-mohs ah leh-ehrr,

④ *a le-er, a le-er.*
ah leh-ehrr, ah leh-ehrr.

Verse 3

Phrase ① *A̶ho-ra va-ya a̶es-cri-bir,*
ah‿oh-rah bah-yah ah‿ehs-kree-beerr,

② *a̶es-cri-bir, a̶es-cri-bir.*
ah‿ehs-kree-beerr, ah‿ehs-kree-beerr.

PRONUNCIATION PRACTICE 29 (CONTINUED)

③ *A_ho-ra va-mos a_es-cri-bir,*
ah‿oh-rah bah-mohs ah‿ehs-kree-beerr,

④ *a_es-cri-bir, a_es-cri-bir.*
ah‿ehs-kree-beerr, ah‿ehs-kree-beerr.

Verse 4

Phrase ① *A_ho-ra va-ya a co-mer,*
ah‿oh-rah bah-yah ah koh-mehrr,

② *a co-mer, a co-mer.*
ah koh-mehrr, ah koh-mehrr.

③ *A_ho-ra va-mos a co-mer,*
ah‿oh-rah bah-mohs ah koh-mehrr,

④ *a co-mer, a co-mer.*
ah koh-mehrr, ah koh-mehrr.

Verse 5

Phrase ① *A_ho-ra va-ya a silbar,*
ah‿oh-rah bah-yah ah seel-bahrr,

② (whistle)...

③ (whistle)...

④ (whistle)...

Verse 6
Phrase ① *A_ho-ra va-ya a re-ír,*
ah_oh-rah bah-yah ah rreh-eerr,

② *ja ja ja, ja ja ja.*
hah hah hah, hah hah hah.

③ *A_ho-ra va-mos ja ja ja,*
ah_oh-rah bah-mohs hah hah hah,

④ *ja ja ja, ja ja ja.*
hah hah hah, hah hah hah.

Verse 7
Phrase ① *A_ho-ra va-ya a bai-lar,*
ah_oh-rah bah-yah ah bah_ee-lahrr,

② *a bai-lar, a bai-lar.*
ah bah_ee-lahrr, ah bah_ee-lahrr.

③ *A_ho-ra va-mos a bai-lar,*
ah_oh-rah bah-mohs ah bah_ee-lahrr,

④ *a bai-lar, a bai-lar.*
ah bah_ee-lahrr, ah bah_ee-lahrr.

Verse 8
Phrase ① *A_ho-ra va-ya a sal-tar,*
ah_oh-rah bah-yah ah sahl-tahrr,

② *a sal-tar, a sal-tar.*
ah sahl-tahrr, ah sahl-tahrr.

● PRONUNCIATION PRACTICE 29 (CONTINUED)

③ *A_ho-ra va-mos a sal-tar,*
ah_oh-rah bah-mohs ah sahl-tahrr,

④ *a sal-tar, a sal-tar.*
ah sahl-tahrr, ah sahl-tahrr.

Verse 9

Phrase ① *A_ho-ra va-ya a ron-car,*
ah_oh-rah bah-yah ah rrohn-kahrr,

② *a ron-car, a ron-car.*
ah rrohn-kahrr, ah rrohn-kahrr.

③ *A_ho-ra va-mos a ron-car,*
ah_oh-rah bah-mohs ah rrohn-kahrr,

④ *a ron-car, a ron-car.*
ah rrohn-kahrr, ah rrohn-kahrr.

Verse 10

Phrase ① *A_ho-ra va-ya a_a-plau-dir,*
ah_oh-rah bah-yah ah-plah_oo-deerr,

② *a_a-plau-dir, a_a-plau-dir.*
ah-plah_oo-deerr, ah-plah_oo-deerr.

③ *A_ho-ra va-mos a_a-plau-dir,*
ah_oh-rah bah-mohs ah-plah_oo-deerr,

④ *a_a-plau-dir, a_a-plau-dir.*
ah-plah_oo-deerr, ah-plah_oo-deerr.

Rinsho, rinsho

Japanese Folk Song

Verse 1

Phrase ① *Rin-sho, rin-sho, i-chi rin-sho;*
rreen-shaw, rreen-shaw, ee-chee rreen-shaw;

② *Na-mo i-chi rin-sho,*
nah-moh ee-chee rreen-shaw,

Verse 2

Phrase ① *Rin-sho, rin-sho, ni rin-sho;*
rreen-shaw, rreen-shaw, nee rreen-shaw;

② *Na-mo ni rin-sho,*
nah-moh nee rreen-shaw,

Verse 3

Phrase ① *Rin-sho, rin-sho, san rin-sho;*
rreen-shaw, rreen-shaw, sah(n) rreen-shaw;

② *Na-mo san rin-sho,*
nah-moh sah(n) rreen-shaw,

Verse 4

Phrase ① *Rin-sho, rin-sho, yon rin-sho;*
rreen-shaw, rreen-shaw, yawn rreen-shaw;

② *Na-mo yon rin-sho,*
nah-moh yawn rreen-shaw,

Verse 5

Phrase ① *Rin-sho, rin-sho, go rin-sho;*
rreen-shaw, rreen-shaw, gaw rreen-shaw;

② *Na-mo go rin-sho,*
nah-moh gaw rreen-shaw,

Refrain: ① Ko-re a-ga ri!
koh-reh ah-gah rree!

PRONUNCIATION PRACTICE 31

Juanito (Little Johnny)

Children's Song from Spain

Verse 1

Phrase ① *Juan-i-to, cuan-do bai-la,*
whahn-ee-toh, kwahn-doh bah‿ee-lah,

② *bai-la, bai-la, bai-la*
bah‿ee-lah, bah‿ee-lah, bah‿ee-lah

③ *Juan-i-to, cuan-do bai-la,*
whahn-ee-toh, kwahn-doh bah‿ee-lah,

④ *bai-la con la ma-no*
bah‿ee-lah kohn lah mah-noh

⑤ *con la ma-no, ma-no, ma-no.*
kohn lah mah-noh, mah-noh, mah-noh.

⑥ *¡Ay qué bien bai-la Juan-i-to!*
ah‿ee keh byehn bah‿ee-lah whahn-ee-toh!

Verse 2

Phrase ① *Juan-i-to, cuan-do bai-la,*
whahn-ee-toh, kwahn-doh bah‿ee-lah,

② *bai-la, bai-la, bai-la*
bah‿ee-lah, bah‿ee-lah, bah‿ee-lah

③ *Juan-i-to, cuan-do bai-la,*
whahn-ee-toh, kwahn-doh bah‿ee-lah,

④ *bai-la con el de-di-to.*
bah‿ee-lah kohn ehl deh-dee-toh.

⑤ *con el de-di-to, di-to, di-to.*
kohn ehl deh-dee-toh, dee-toh, dee-toh.

⑥ *¡Ay qué bien bai-la Juan-i-to!*
ah‿ee keh byehn bah‿ee-lah whahn-ee-toh!

Verse 3

Phrase ① *Juan-i-to, cuan-do bai-la,*
whahn-ee-toh, kwahn-doh bah‿ee-lah,

② *bai-la, bai-la, bai-la*
bah‿ee-lah, bah‿ee-lah, bah‿ee-lah

③ *Juan-i-to, cuan-do bai-la,*
whahn-ee-toh, kwahn-doh bah‿ee-lah,

④ *bai-la con el pie*
bah‿ee-lah kohn ehl pee‿yeh

⑤ *con el pie, con el pie, pie, pie.*
kohn ehl pee‿yeh, kohn ehl pee‿yeh, pee‿yeh, pee‿yeh.

⑥ *¡Ay qué bien bai-la Juan-i-to!*
ah‿ee keh byehn bah‿ee-lah whahn-ee-toh!

Verse 4

Phrase ① *Juan-i-to, cuan-do bai-la,*
whahn-ee-toh, kwahn-doh bah‿ee-lah,

② *bai-la, bai-la, bai-la*
bah‿ee-lah, bah‿ee-lah, bah‿ee-lah

③ *Juan-i-to, cuan-do bai-la,*
whahn-ee-toh, kwahn-doh bah‿ee-lah,

④ *bai-la con la ca-be-za,*
bah‿ee-lah kohn lah kah-beh-sah,

⑤ con la ca-be-za, be-za, be-za.
kohn lah kah-beh-sah, beh-sah, beh-sah.

⑥ *¡Ay qué bien bai-la Juan-i-to!*
ah_ee keh byehn bah_ee-lah whahn-ee-toh!

Verse 5

Phrase ① *Juan-i-to, cuan-do bai-la,*
whahn-ee-toh, kwahn-doh bah_ee-lah,

② *bai-la, bai-la, bai-la*
bah_ee-lah, bah_ee-lah, bah_ee-lah

③ *Juan-i-to, cuan-do bai-la,*
whahn-ee-toh, kwahn-doh bah_ee-lah,

④ *bai-la con el hombro,*
bah_ee-lah kohn ehl ohm-broh,

⑤ *con el hombro, hombro, hombro.*
kohn ehl ohm-broh, ohm-broh, ohm-broh.

⑥ *¡Ay qué bien bai-la Juan-i-to!*
ah_ee keh byehn bah_ee-lah whahn-ee-toh!

Verse 6

Phrase ① *Juan-i-to, cuan-do bai-la,*
whahn-ee-toh, kwahn-doh bah_ee-lah,

② *bai-la, bai-la, bai-la*
bah_ee-lah, bah_ee-lah, bah_ee-lah

③ *Juan-i-to, cuan-do bai-la,*
whahn-ee-toh, kwahn-doh bah_ee-lah,

④ *bai-la con el co-do,*
bah‿ee-lah kohn ehl koh-doh,

⑤ *con el co-do, co-do, co-do.*
kohn ehl koh-doh, koh-doh, koh-doh.

⑥ *¡Ay qué bien bai-la Juan-i-to!*
ah‿ee keh byehn bah‿ee-lah whahn-ee-toh!

PRONUNCIATION PRACTICE 32

Uga uga uga (Cake! Cake! Cake!)

Israeli Folk Tune

Phrase ① *U-ga u-ga u-ga*
oo-gah oo-gah oo-gah

② *Ba-ma_a-gal na-chu-ga*
bah-mah_a-gahl nah-hkhoo-gah

③ *Nis-to-ve-va*
nees-toh-veh-vah

④ *kol-ha_o-yam*
kohl-hah_oh-yahm

⑤ *Ad ash-er*
ahd ah-shehr

⑥ *nim-tza ma-kom*
neem-tzah mah-koom

⑦ *La-she-vet la-kum*
lah-sheh-veht lah-koom

⑧ *La-she-vet la-kum*
lah-sheh-veht lah-koom

⑨ *La-she-vet v' la-kum*
lah-sheh-veht veh'lah-koom

Kindergarten, Teacher Edition, page 305

A-41

El día de mamita (Mommy's Day)

Folk Song from Venezuela

Phrase ① *Flo-res del cam-po*
floh-rehs dehl kahm-poh

② *de mil co-lo-res*
deh meel koh-loh-rehs

③ *las ma-nos lle-nas*
lahs mah-nohs yeh-nahs

④ *le lle-va-ré*
leh yeh-vah-reh

⑤ *a mi ma-mi-ta*
ah mee mah-mee-tah

⑥ *hoy en su dí-a*
oi ehn soo dee-ah

⑦ *con un be-si-to*
kohn oon beh-see-toh

⑧ *se las da-ré.*
seh lahs dah-reh.

PRONUNCIATION PRACTICE 34

Phonetic Pronunciation for Choral Singing of Non-English Songs

ah	as in f<u>a</u>ther	(m)	French nasal <u>m</u>, not articulated as a distinct letter but as an open nasal sound
ah‿ee	as a more pleasant long *i* sound (tall *ah* sounded for duration, with a hint of *ee* at close)	n	as in <u>n</u>ote
aw	as in <u>awe</u>	(n)	French nasal <u>n</u>, not articulated as a distinct letter, but as an open nasal sound.
eh‿ee	as in d<u>ay</u> (tall *eh* sounded for duration, with a hint of *ee* at close)	(ng)	as in sa<u>ng</u> (sometimes sounded as a prolonged nasal tone)
b	as in <u>b</u>utton	oh	as in t<u>o</u>ne
ch	as in <u>ch</u>urch	oo	as in sp<u>oo</u>n
d	as in <u>d</u>ad	ow	as in p<u>ow</u>der
dj	as in ju<u>dg</u>e	p	as in <u>p</u>at
ee	as in s<u>ee</u>d	r	as in <u>r</u>an
eh	as in l<u>e</u>t	(r)	as in tu<u>r</u>n (combined with another vowel sound in German)
ew	used for French u (pronounce a bright *ee* and round the lips as if to whistle)	rr	rolled <u>r</u>
f	as in <u>f</u>ace	rrrr	extended trilled <u>r</u>
g	as in <u>g</u>oat	s	as in <u>s</u>ong
h	as in <u>h</u>at	t	as in <u>t</u>ell
hkh	guttural, aspirant <u>h</u> of German and Hebrew <u>ch</u>	th	as in <u>th</u>at
ih	as in f<u>i</u>t	thh	as in fea<u>th</u>er
I	as in l<u>i</u>ght (a harsh *i* sound, where possible an *ah‿ee* has been suggested for singing the I sound.)	uh	as in <u>u</u>p
		v	as in <u>v</u>an
k	as in <u>k</u>ite	w	as in <u>w</u>ay
l	as in <u>l</u>et	wh	as in <u>wh</u>at
ll	prolonged <u>l</u> sound	y	as in <u>y</u>es (not a vowel sound)
m	as in <u>m</u>an	z	as in <u>z</u>one
		zh	as in a<u>z</u>ure

Teacher Notes

ASSESSMENT
Table of Contents

ASSESSMENT

ASSESSMENT 1: UNIT 1

What Do You Know?

Ways We Move

Some movements help you travel from place to place.

Which of these movements help you travel?

Circle these movements.

1.

2.

3.

4.

Kindergarten, Teacher Edition, page 28

ASSESSMENT 1: UNIT 1 (CONTINUED)

What Do You Hear? 1   Loud and Soft

Circle the roaring lion if you hear loud music.

Circle the mouse if you hear soft music.

1.

2.

3.

4.

ASSESSMENT

ASSESSMENT 1: UNIT 1 (CONTINUED)

What You Can Do

Create a Sound Story of High and Low

These things make sounds.

Make each of these sounds.

Will you use your high voice or your low voice?

1. ↑ ↓

2. ↑ ↓

3. ↑ ↓

4. ↑ ↓

5. ↑ ↓

6. ↑ ↓

7. ↑ ↓

8. ↑ ↓

ASSESSMENT 2: UNIT 2

Review, Assess, Perform, Create

What Do You Know?

Loud and Soft Moves

What movements are these people doing?

Is the movement loud or soft?

Circle the movements that are soft.

ASSESSMENT 2: UNIT 2 (CONTINUED)

What Do You Hear? 2A   **High and Low**

High Voice? Low Voice?

Circle the baby mouse if you hear a high voice.

Circle the bear if you hear a low voice.

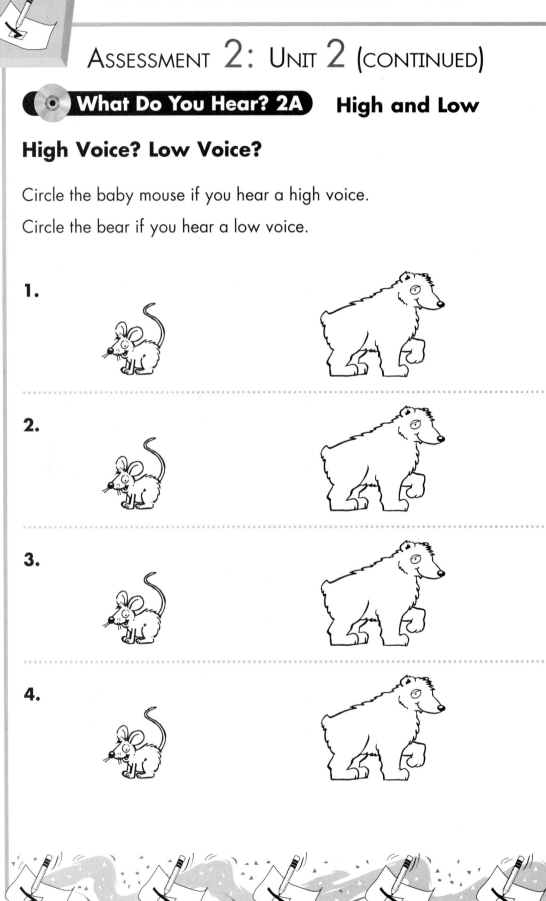

1.

2.

3.

4.

ASSESSMENT 2: UNIT 2 (CONTINUED)

What Do You Hear? 2B **Sing, Speak, Shout, Whisper**

We can sing, speak, shout, and whisper.

Circle the voice that you hear.

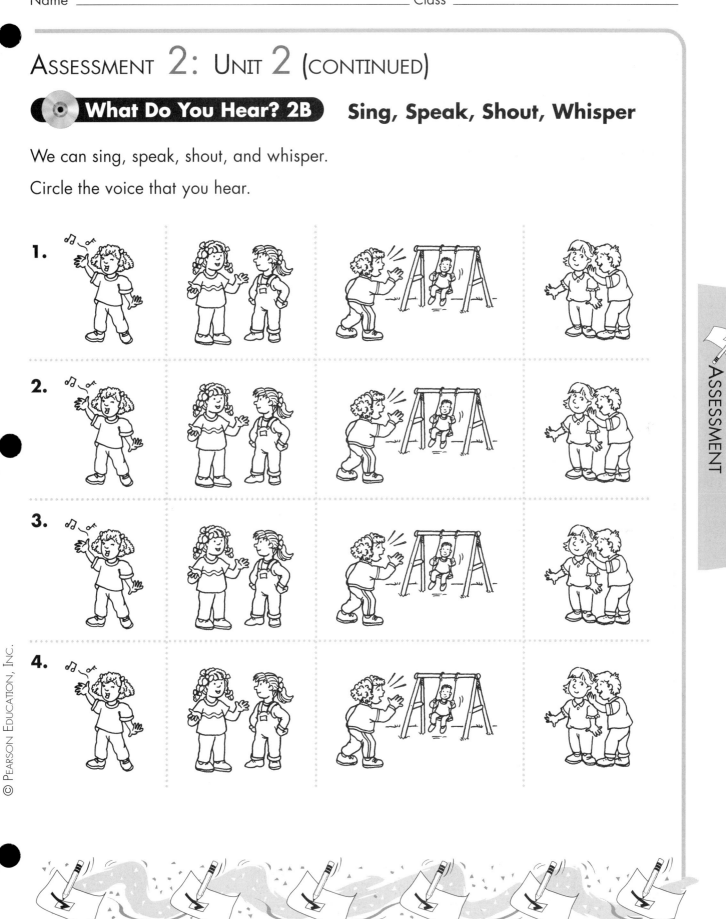

ASSESSMENT 2: UNIT 2 (CONTINUED)

What You Can Do

Move on the Steady Beat

Listen to the words.

Circle the movement that they tell you to do.

Do this movement on the steady beat.

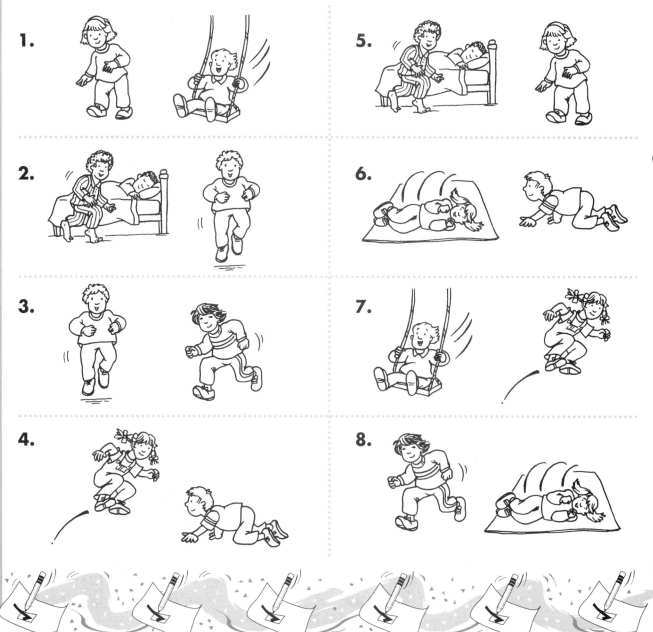

1.

2.

3.

4.

5.

6.

7.

8.

ASSESSMENT 3: UNIT 3

Review, Assess, Perform, Create

What Do You Know?

On the Go, Fast or Slow?

The animals are going to a party.

Which animals will get there quickly?

Circle the animals that move slowly.

ASSESSMENT

Assessment 3: Unit 3 (continued)

What Do You Hear? 3A   Fast and Slow

Circle the turtle if you hear slow music.

Circle the dog if you hear fast music.

1.

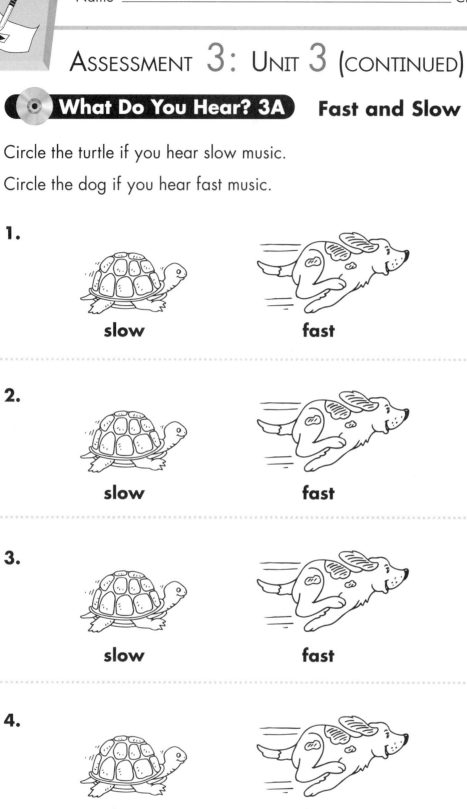

slow   fast

2.

slow   fast

3.

slow   fast

4.

slow   fast

Kindergarten, Teacher Edition, page 84

ASSESSMENT 3: UNIT 3 (CONTINUED)

What Do You Hear? 3B   **Nature Sounds and Machine Sounds**

Circle the bird if you hear a nature sound.

Circle the vacuum cleaner if you hear a machine sound.

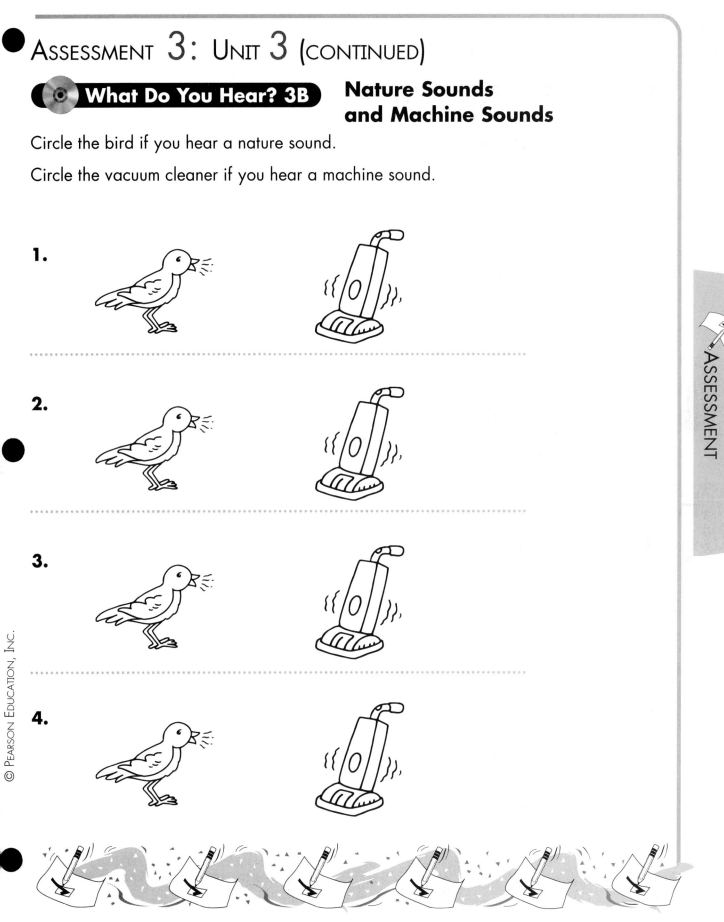

1.

2.

3.

4.

ASSESSMENT

© PEARSON EDUCATION, INC.

Assessment 3: Unit 3 (continued)

What You Can Do

Create a Bus Ride Sound Story

Many things on a bus make sound.

Make each of these sounds.

What instrument will you choose?

1.

4.

2.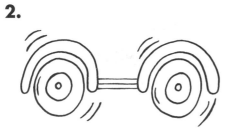

5.

3.

6.

ASSESSMENT 4: UNIT 4

Review, Assess, Perform, Create

What Do You Know?

Crawling Up and Down

Fuzzy Caterpillar moves up and then down.

Does he move up or down next?

Circle the arrow that shows how Fuzzy moves.

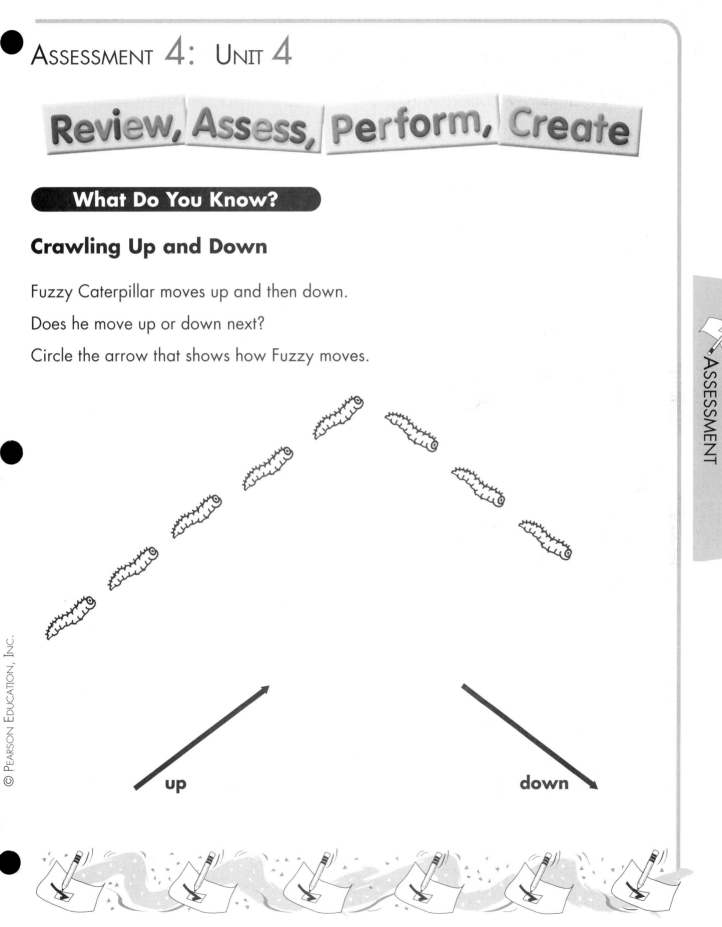

up

down

ASSESSMENT

ASSESSMENT 4: UNIT 4 (CONTINUED)

What Do You Hear? 4   **Upward and Downward**

Circle the arrow that shows the way the music moves.

Does the music move upward or downward?

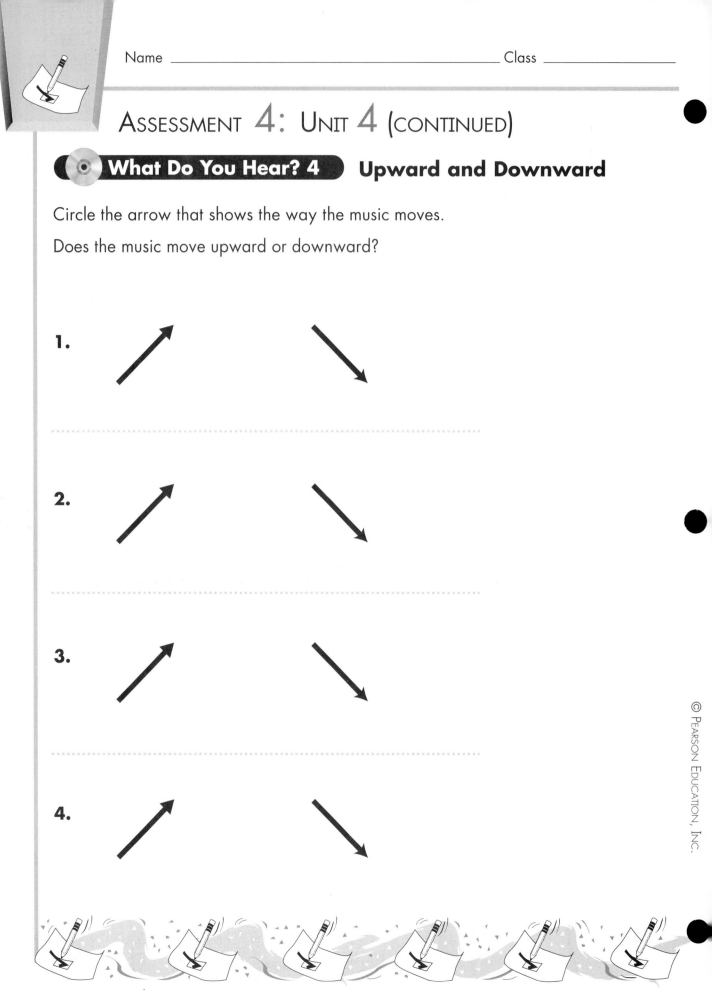

Kindergarten, Teacher Edition, page 112

● Assessment 4: Unit 4 (continued)

What You Can Do

Beats in the Moonlight

Tap the moons on the beat.

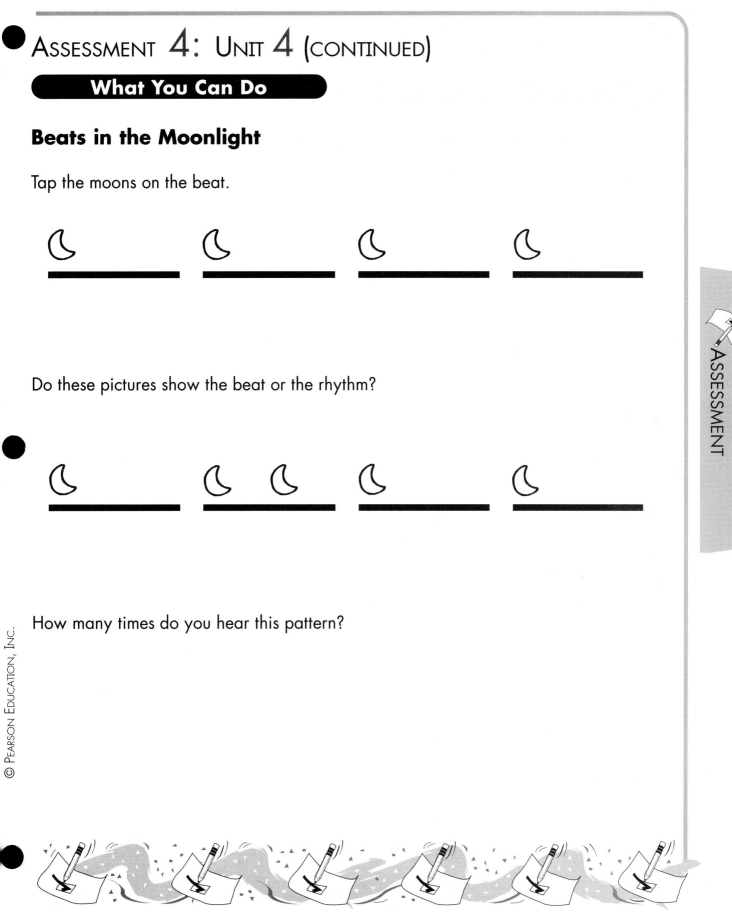

Do these pictures show the beat or the rhythm?

How many times do you hear this pattern?

ASSESSMENT

ASSESSMENT 5: UNIT 5

Review, Assess, Perform, Create

What Do You Know?

Long and Short Frogs

How many long frogs do you see?

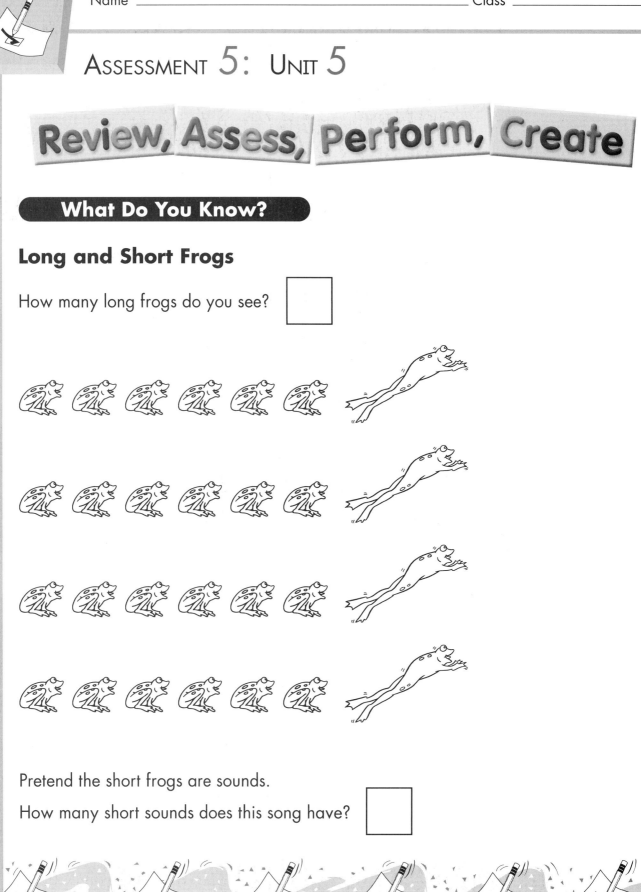

Pretend the short frogs are sounds.

How many short sounds does this song have?

Kindergarten, Teacher Edition, page 140

ASSESSMENT 5: UNIT 5 (CONTINUED)

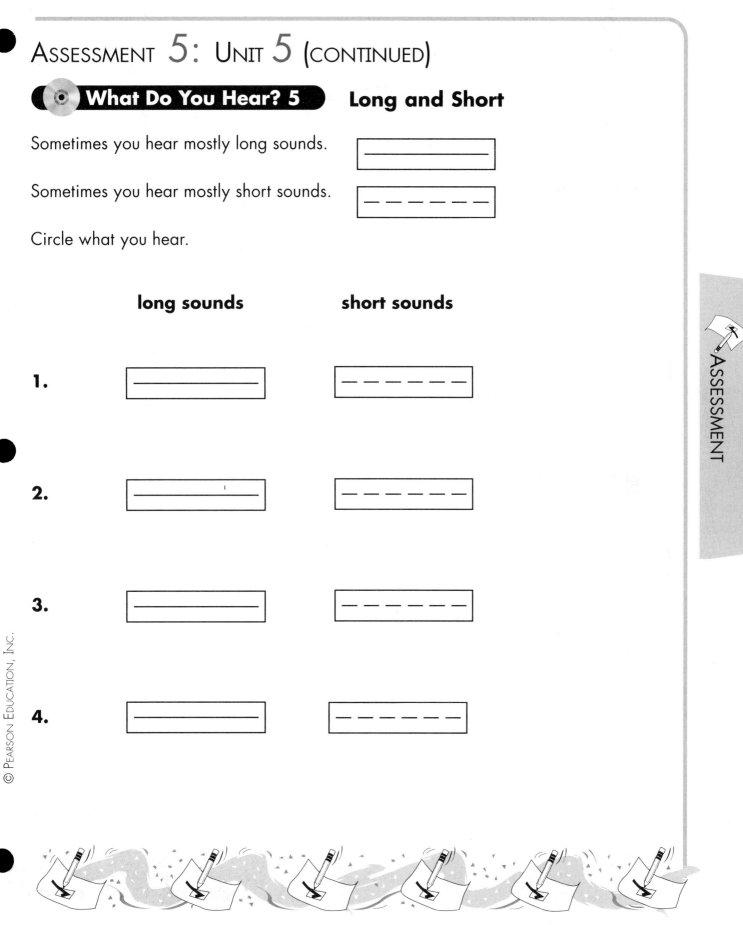

What Do You Hear? 5   Long and Short

Sometimes you hear mostly long sounds.

Sometimes you hear mostly short sounds.

Circle what you hear.

long sounds   **short sounds**

1.

2.

3.

4.

ASSESSMENT

ASSESSMENT 5: UNIT 5 (CONTINUED)

What You Can Do

Create a Giddy Up Sound Story

Create sounds to tell this story.

What instruments will you use?

Giddy up horsey,

Don't say stop,

Just let your feet

Go clippety clop and hippity hop;

Giddy up,

We're homeward bound.

ASSESSMENT 6: UNIT 6

Review, Assess, Perform, Create

What Do You Know?

Counting the Sounds on the Beat

Circle the beats that have two sounds.

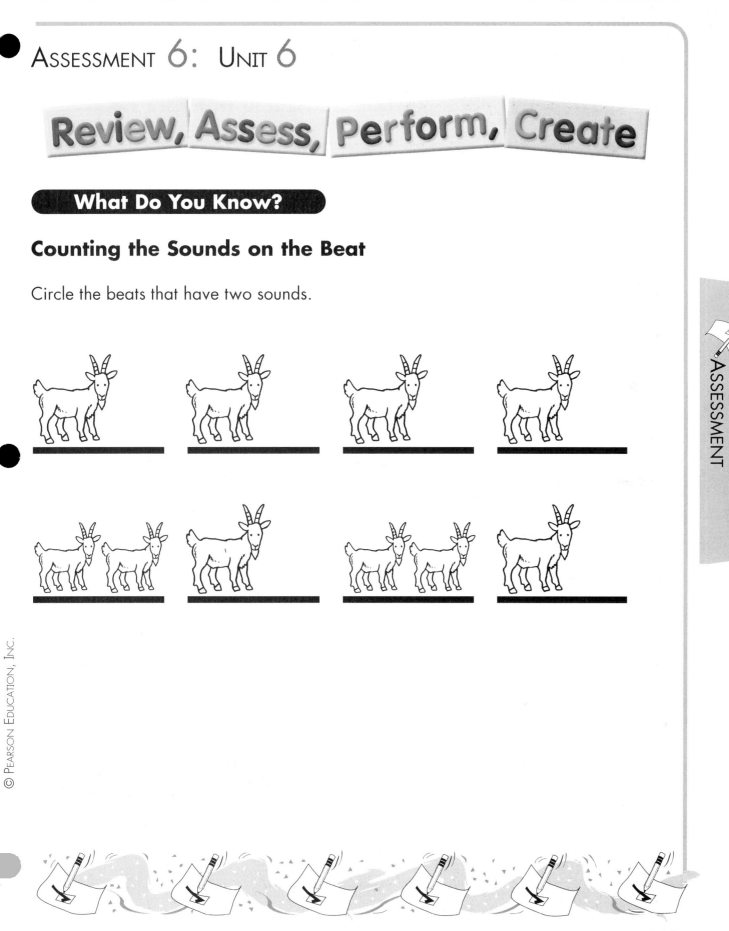

ASSESSMENT 6: UNIT 6 (CONTINUED)

What Do You Hear? 6   Same and Different Parts

Listen to these musical parts.

Are these parts the same or different?

Circle what you hear.

Same	**Different**

1.

2.

3.

4.

Kindergarten, Teacher Edition, page 168

ASSESSMENT 6: UNIT 6 (CONTINUED)

What You Can Do

Read a Melody Pattern

How many times does the frog sing his pattern?

Move a hand to show this pattern.

Sing the frog's pattern.

Assessment: Introduction

Introduction for the Music Teacher

Checklists

Checklists are provided for performance skills (singing, playing instruments, reading, improvising, moving) and non-performance skills (composing/arranging/notating, listening). Have individual children demonstrate each of the items on the checklists. Guide the children in selecting music and tasks that will permit them to meet all of the goals outlined in the checklists.

You may consider assembling small ensembles in which children with different skill levels all perform a given piece together, but with children playing parts that are appropriate for their various skill levels. When reviewing children's work, continue to refer to the items on the checklists and point out ways their work does or does not meet each of the criteria. For children who do not perform as well as they are capable, provide opportunities to perform small sections of their pieces again. Have the children pay attention to one or two specific points that will improve their work. In this way, assessment becomes an important and contributing part of the learning process.

Rubrics

The rubrics are designed to be used together with the checklists. The goal of performance skills is for all children to perform well, regardless of the difficulty of the material they perform. The goal of non-performance skills is for all children to demonstrate competence, regardless of the difficulty of the composing, arranging, and listening tasks that they are assigned. Of course, some items on the checklists are more important than others, but all of them work together to create successful, expressive music performances, compositions, or informed listening experiences. If you wish to summarize your evaluations of the children's performances or work in a way that allows you to place each child or small group on a graded scale, you may use the rubrics for describing their performances or work.

ASSESSMENT: PERFORMANCE SKILLS

Singing

Checklist for Singing
❑ Posture is upright and relaxed.
❑ Jaw and mouth are relaxed and open.
❑ Breath is inhaled with natural, relaxed expansion of the body.
❑ Tone is free, open, and even throughout range.
❑ Singing is accurate and in tune.
❑ Rhythm is precise and sung with inflection.
❑ Diction is clear (all words are understood).
❑ Volume level is balanced with other members of the ensemble.
❑ Dynamic and rhythmic variations are used to create expressive effects.

Rubric for Singing
❑ **Fluent** The child sings with fluency and ease. There are few errors. All items on the checklist are consistently demonstrated. The performance is confident, beautiful, and expressive.

❑ **Competent** The child sings with relative ease, but several errors or hesitations are present. Most items on the checklist are consistently demonstrated. The performance is confident and expressive.

❑ **More Practice Needed** The child has difficulty performing evenly and in time. Hesitations and errors are clearly evident. Only some of the checklist items are demonstrated. The performance does not convey the expressive intent of the piece performed.

ASSESSMENT

ASSESSMENT: PERFORMANCE SKILLS

Playing Instruments

Checklist for Playing Instruments
- ❑ Posture is upright and relaxed.
- ❑ Instruments, sticks, and mallets (when used) are held loosely and comfortably.
- ❑ Arms, hands, and fingers move easily (no tension evident).
- ❑ Playing motion is efficient and smooth.
- ❑ Instrument tone is open, resonant, and even.
- ❑ Notes are performed accurately and in tune.
- ❑ Rhythm is accurate and precise.
- ❑ Tempo is steady and even.
- ❑ Volume level is balanced with other members of the ensemble.
- ❑ Dynamic and rhythmic variations are used to create expressive effects.

Rubric for Playing Instruments
- ❑ **Fluent** The child plays with fluency and ease. There are few errors. All items on the checklist are consistently demonstrated. The performance is confident, beautiful, and expressive.

- ❑ **Competent** The child plays with relative ease, but several errors or hesitations are present. Most items on the checklist are consistently demonstrated. The performance is confident and expressive.

- ❑ **More Practice Needed** The child has difficulty performing evenly and in time. Hesitations and errors are clearly evident. Only some of the checklist items are demonstrated. The performance does not convey the expressive intent of the piece performed.

ASSESSMENT: PERFORMANCE SKILLS

Reading

Checklist for Reading
*❑ Selects appropriate tempo at which to perform unfamiliar music.
*❑ Identifies passages that are not immediately interpretable or technically difficult.
❑ Rehearses difficult or unfamiliar elements in isolation.
❑ Pitches are performed accurately.
❑ Rhythm is accurate and precise.
❑ Rhythm is performed with appropriate inflection.
❑ Style of articulation (if applicable) is accurate and consistent.
❑ Dynamic levels are accurate.
❑ Tempo is steady and even when appropriate.
❑ Rhythmic and dynamic variations are used to create expressive effects.

* Refer to tasks involved in learning unfamiliar music.

Rubric for Reading
❑ **Fluent** The child reads with fluency and ease. There are few errors. All items on the checklist are consistently demonstrated. The performance is confident, beautiful, and expressive.

❑ **Competent** The child reads with relative ease, but several errors or hesitations are present. Most items on the checklist are consistently demonstrated. The performance is confident and expressive.

❑ **More Practice Needed** The child has difficulty performing evenly and in time. Hesitations and errors are clearly evident. Only some of the checklist items are demonstrated. The performance does not convey the expressive intent of the piece performed.

ASSESSMENT

ASSESSMENT: PERFORMANCE SKILLS

Moving and Improvising

Checklist for Moving
❑ Weight of the body is balanced and secure.
❑ Limbs move easily and without unnecessary tension.
❑ Movements depict the style of music (for example, rhythm, articulation).
❑ Movements are coordinated with the pulse of the music (if applicable).
❑ Changes in movements appropriately mirror changes in the music.
❑ Sizes and distances of movements are appropriate for the occasion and location
(for example, on a dance floor, in a circle with classmates, or seated in a chair).

Checklist for Improvising
❑ Notes are grouped in discernible phrases.
❑ Repetition of melodic motives is used to extend and elaborate phrases.
❑ Individual phrases are unified by consistency and continuity.
❑ Phrases are organized with clear, balanced antecedents and consequents.
❑ Harmonic motion (when harmony is present) is logical.
❑ Dynamic and rhythmic variations are used to create expressive effects.
❑ Musical effects are consistent with the improviser's intent.

Rubric for Moving and Improvising
❑ **Fluent** The child moves or improvises with fluency and ease. There are few
errors. All items on the checklist are consistently demonstrated. The performance
is confident, beautiful, and expressive.

❑ **Competent** The child moves or improvises with relative ease, but several errors or
hesitations are present. Most items on the checklist are consistently demonstrated.
The performance is confident and expressive.

❑ **More Practice Needed** The child has difficulty performing evenly and in time.
Hesitations and errors are clearly evident. Only some of the checklist items are
demonstrated. The performance does not convey the expressive intent of the
piece performed.

Assessment: Non-Performance Skills

Composing/Arranging/Notating

Checklist for Composing/Arranging/Notating
❏ Instrument timbres and voice parts are combined effectively.
❏ Notes are grouped in phrases.
❏ Repetition of melodic motives is used to extend and elaborate phrases.
❏ Individual phrases are unified by consistency and continuity.
❏ Phrases are organized with clear, balanced antecedents and consequents.
❏ Harmonic motion (when harmony is present) is logical.
❏ Part-writing (if applicable) follows the conventions of the style of composition.
❏ Dynamic and rhythmic variations are used to create expressive effects.
❏ Musical effects are consistent with the intent of the composer or arranger.
❏ Musical sounds are accurately transcribed using formal, informal, or invented notation.
❏ Notation is clear and readable by others.

Rubric for Composing/Arranging/Notating
❏ **Fluent** The composition or arrangement is expressive, beautiful, and consistent with the intent of the composer or arranger. All items on the checklist are consistently demonstrated.

❏ **Competent** The composition or arrangement is well organized and consistent with the intent of the composer or arranger. Most items on the checklist are consistently demonstrated.

❏ **More Practice Needed** The composition or arrangement is somewhat organized and may not be consistent with the intent of the composer or arranger. Only some of the checklist items are demonstrated.

ASSESSMENT

ASSESSMENT: NON-PERFORMANCE SKILLS

Listening

Checklist for Listening

The first four items on this checklist pertain to behavior while listening; the remaining four pertain to auditory discriminations explained after listening.

❑ Remains quiet (when appropriate) while listening to live or recorded music.

❑ Remains stationary (when appropriate) while listening to live or recorded music.

❑ Moves appropriately while listening to music (for example, tapping to the beat, dancing) in social settings where movement is appropriate.

❑ Acknowledges performers with applause (when appropriate).

❑ Describes the timbres of musical tones and labels instruments and voice parts.

❑ Describes the formal organization of sounds (for example, the use of repetition, melodic contour, motivic development)

❑ Describes the emotional effects that the music elicits from self and others.

❑ Describes possible functions of the music in cultural contexts.

Rubric for Listening Discrimination

❑ **Fluent** All aspects of the music are accurately described, and the observations about the music are informative and interesting. All items on the checklist are consistently demonstrated.

❑ **Competent** Most aspects of the music are accurately described, and the observations about the music are informative. Most items on the checklist are consistently demonstrated.

❑ **More Practice Needed** Aspects of the music are described, but some important information is inaccurate or omitted. Only some of the checklist items are demonstrated.

Assessment Answer Key

Unit 1:

What Do You Know?

These movements help us get from place to place: walking, skipping, running, and tiptoeing.

What Do You Hear? 1

1. Loud—Sousa: *Stars and Stripes Forever*
2. Soft—Debussy: *Nocturnes*, "Nuages"
3. Loud—Copland: *The Red Pony*, "Circus Music"
4. Soft—Stravinsky: *Firebird Suite*, "Berceuse"

Unit 2:

What Do You Know?

The *soft movements* are done by the sleepy child walking, the child doing a two-finger clap, the child tiptoeing, and the ballerinas dancing on tiptoes.

What Do You Hear? 2A

1. Low—the Giant from "Jack and the Beanstalk"
2. High—the Three Pigs from "The Three Little Pigs"
3. High—the Gingerbread Man from "The Gingerbread Man"
4. Low—the Wolf from "The Three Little Pigs"

What Do You Hear? 2B

1. Sing—"Down By the Bay"
2. Speak—"Shake-'n'-Bake a Jelly" (poem)
3. Shout—*The Sounds of the Circus*
4. Whisper—*Louds and Softs of the Seasons* (montage)

Unit 3:

What Do You Know?

The animals that move quickly are the horse running, the squirrel scurrying, and the dog chasing the cat. The animals that move slowly are the turtle crawling, the worm slithering, and the snail crawling.

What Do You Hear? 3A

1. Slow—Gershwin: *Preludes for Piano, No. 2*
2. Fast—Stravinsky: *Pulcinella Suite*, "Tarantella"
3. Fast—Mussorgsky: *Pictures at an Exhibition*, "Ballet of the Unhatched Chicks"
4. Slow—Beethoven: *Minuet in G Major*

What Do You Hear? 3B

1. Nature—Rain Sounds
2. Machine—*Machine Music*, "Garbage truck"
3. Machine Music—"*Los trencitos*"
4. Nature—*Bird Calls, Bird Songs*, "Black-Capped Chickadee"

Unit 4:

What Do You Know?

Measure 1 moves upward; measure 2 moves downward.

What Do You Hear? 4

1. Upward—Cello
2. Downward—Trumpet
3. Upward—Flute
4. Downward—Bassoon

Unit 5:

What Do You Know?

There are four long frogs. The song has twenty-four short sounds.

What Do You Hear? 5

1. Long—Mendelssohn: *A Midsummer Night's Dream*, "Nocturne"
2. Short—Cowell: *Six Ings*, "Scooting"
3. Short—Handel: *Water Music Suite*, "Bourrée"
4. Long—Bizet: *L'Arlesiénne Suite, No. 1*, "Adagietto"

Unit 6:

What Do You Know?

Beats 5 and 7, which are shown in the second row, have two sounds.

What Do You Hear? 6

1. Different—"*Vamos a hacer la ronda*" (Let's Make a Circle)
2. Different—"Rig-a-Jig-Jig"
3. Same—"Bear Dance"
4. Same—"Goin' to the Fair"

What You Can Do

The A-B-F♯ pitch pattern in "On a Log, Mister Frog" occurs three times.

ASSESSMENT

Teacher Notes

GRAPHIC ORGANIZERS

Table of Contents

GRAPHIC ORGANIZER

GRAPHIC ORGANIZER 1

Comparison Chart

Alike	Different

GRAPHIC ORGANIZER 2

Semantic Map

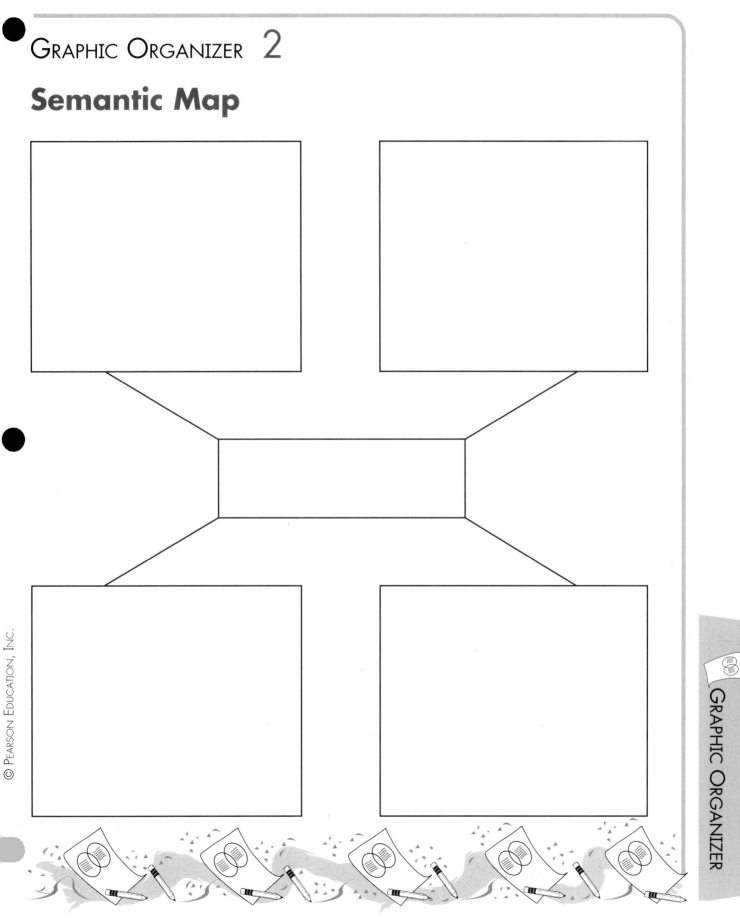

GRAPHIC ORGANIZER

GRAPHIC ORGANIZER 3

Sequence

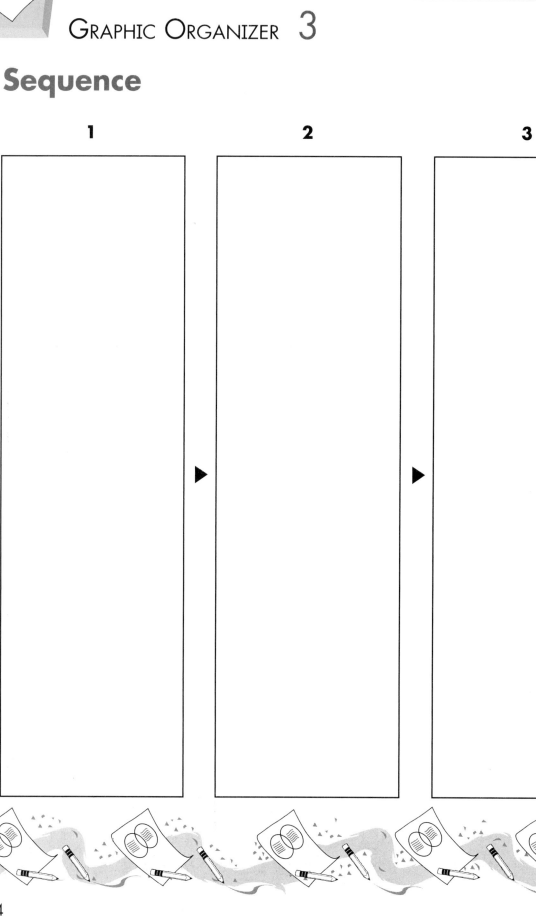

1

2

3

GRAPHIC ORGANIZER 4

Story Map

Title: _____

Beginning:
  Who
  Where
  When

Middle:
  What

End

Graphic Organizer 5

Venn Diagram

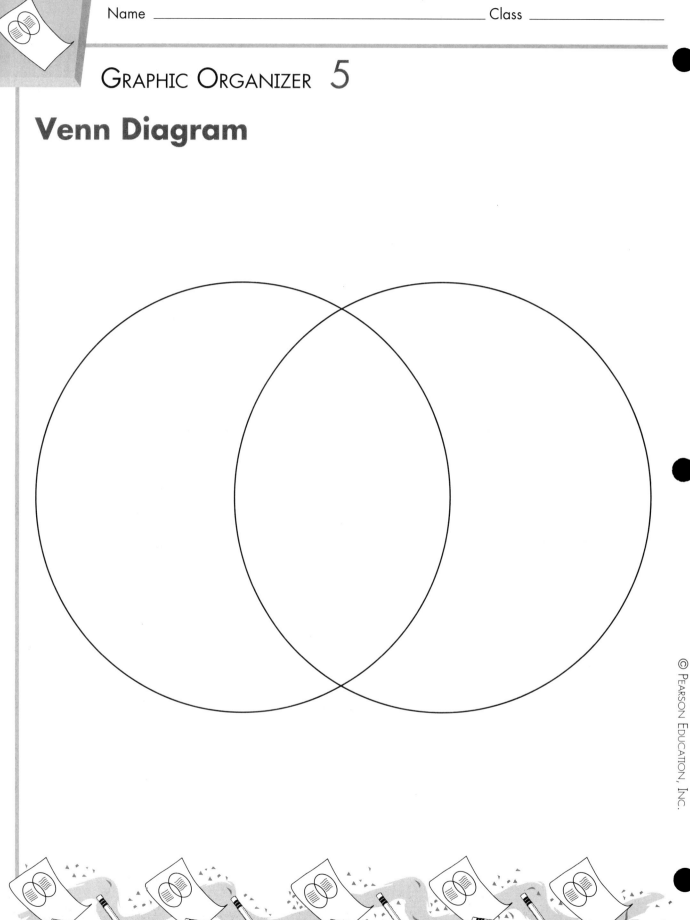

MUSIC READING WORKSHEETS
Table of Contents

Text has been provided on each page so that you may explain to the children what they are to do.

Music Reading Worksheet 1

On the Rainy Day Beat

Tap the pictures on the beat.

Rain on the Green Grass

Traditional Children's Rhyme

MUSIC READING WORKSHEET 2

Knock! Knock! On the Beat

Tap the pictures on the steady beat.

1, 2, 3, 4

Traditional Children's Rhyme

MUSIC READING WORKSHEET 3

Animal Talk High and Low

Make the animal sounds.

Circle the animals that make low sounds.

Three Little Pigs

*Traditional Children's Song
of the United States*

MUSIC READING WORKSHEET 4

On the Bubbly Beat

Tap the bubbles on the beat.

Bubble Gum

Traditional Children's Rhyme

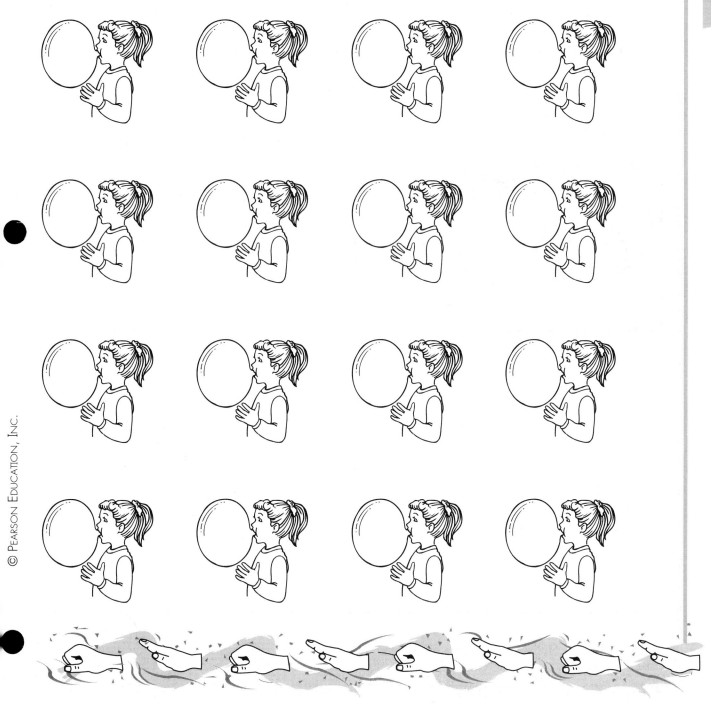

MUSIC READING WORKSHEET 5

Does the Animal Move High or Low?

Listen to each piece of music.

Do you hear high sounds or low sounds?

Circle the animal that makes these sounds.

"The Aviary" and "The Elephant" from Carnival of the Animals

Camille Saint-Saëns

Music Reading Worksheet 6

Andy Pandy High and Low

Tap the pictures on the steady beat. Which sound is lowest?

Andy Pandy

Traditional Game Song

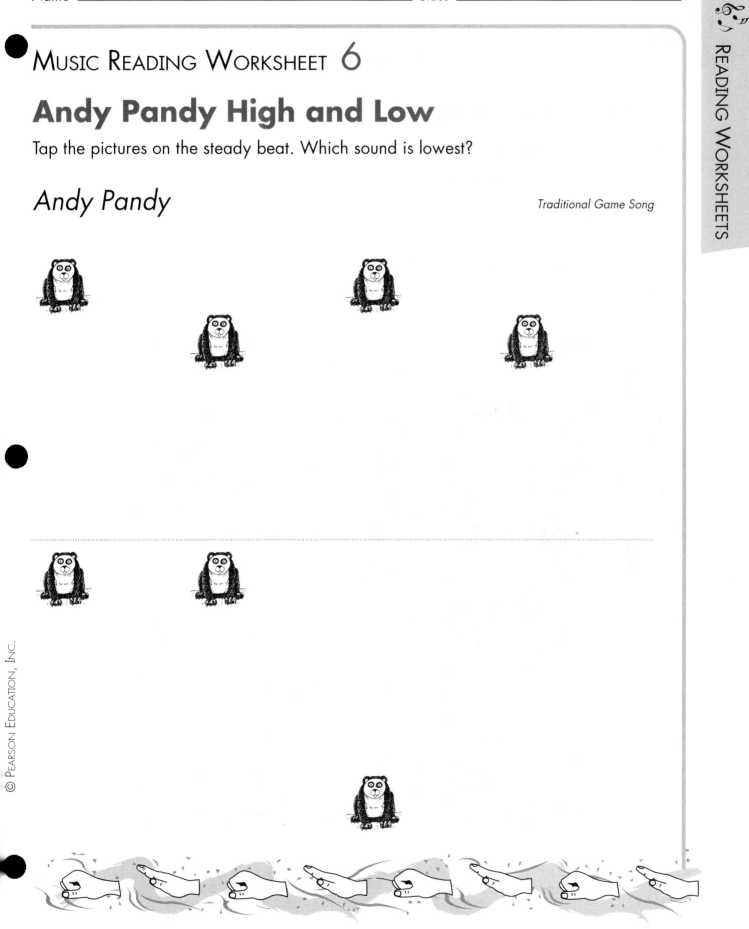

MUSIC READING WORKSHEET 7

Work Beat, Work Rhythm

Tap the stones on the beat.

Tap the corn on the rhythm.

Corn Grinding Song

Native American Folk Melody of the Hopi People

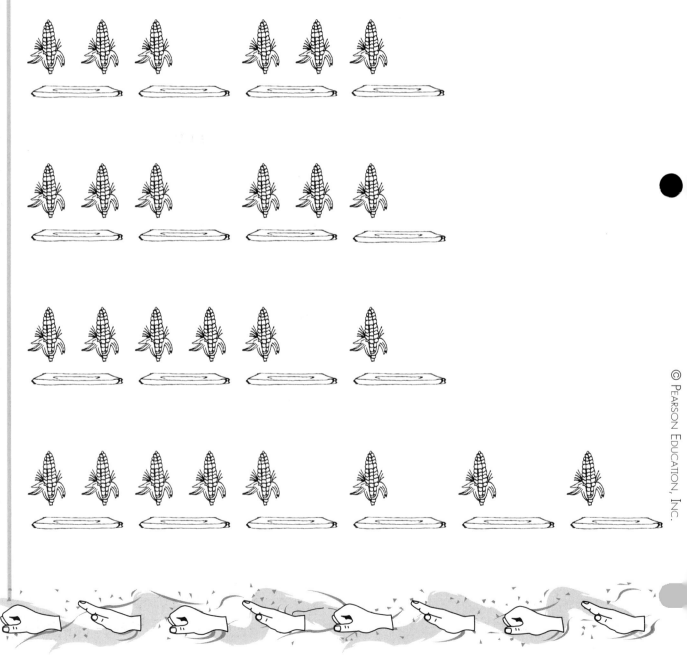

Kindergarten, Teacher Edition, page 66

MUSIC READING WORKSHEET 8

Up the Stairs She Goes

Tap Mary as she moves up the stairs.

Mary Wore Her Red Dress

Folk Song of the United States

MUSIC READING WORKSHEET 9

Following the Bee As It Moves

Tap the bee as it flies down the hive.

Busy Buzzy Bee

*Traditional Children's Song
of the United States*

MUSIC READING WORKSHEET 10

Spider Spins on the Beat

Tap the rhythm on the spiders.

Which sound is different?

Little Spider

Children's Song from Hungary

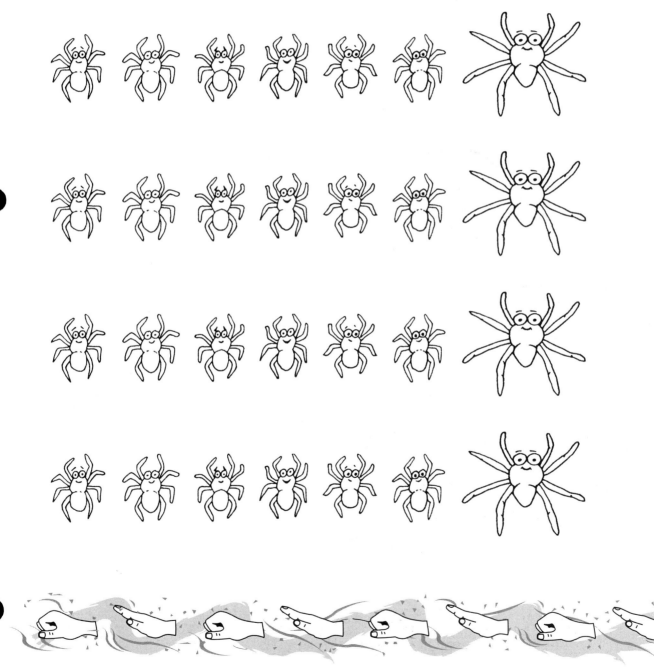

MUSIC READING WORKSHEET 11

Bright Candles, Silent Candles

Tap the candles with the music.

Which candles have no sound?

Pretend to blow out the silent candles.

Ég a gyertya (Candle Burning Bright)

Children's Song from Hungary

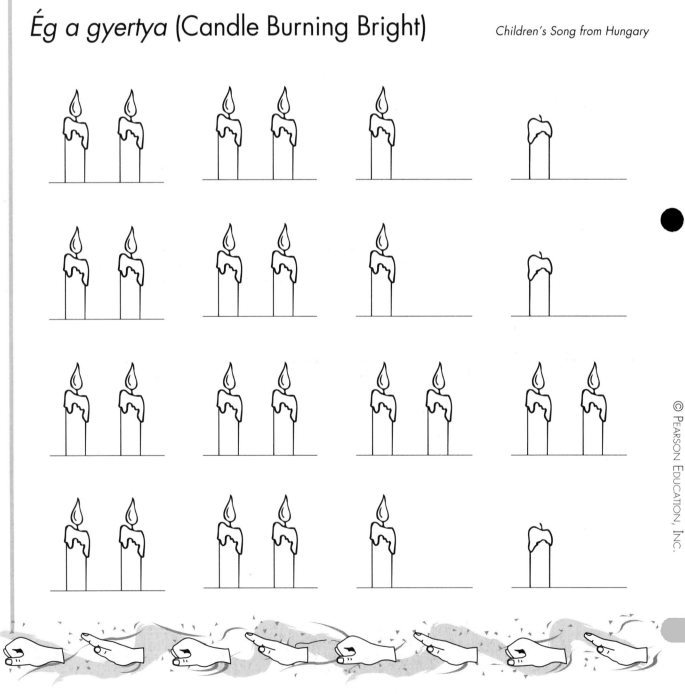

Kindergarten, Teacher Edition, page 96

Music Reading Worksheet 12

An Up-and-Down Sheep Song

Tap the sheep as it moves up and down.

Baa-Baa Black Sheep

Nursery Rhyme from England
Arranged by Mary Ellen Junda

MUSIC READING WORKSHEET 13

Up and Down My Window

Which birds show the *bluebird* pattern?

Bluebird, Bluebird

Game Song from the United States

D-14

Kindergarten, Teacher Edition, page 104

MUSIC READING WORKSHEET 14

Long Dog, Short Dog, Good Dog, You!

Tap the pattern on the dog bones.

Circle the longest dog bones.

Old Blue (Refrain)

Mountain Song of the Southern United States

MUSIC READING WORKSHEET 15

Snail Dances Up and Down

Tap the snail as it moves.

Does it move mostly up or mostly down?

El caracol (The Snail's Dance)

Children's Song from Spain

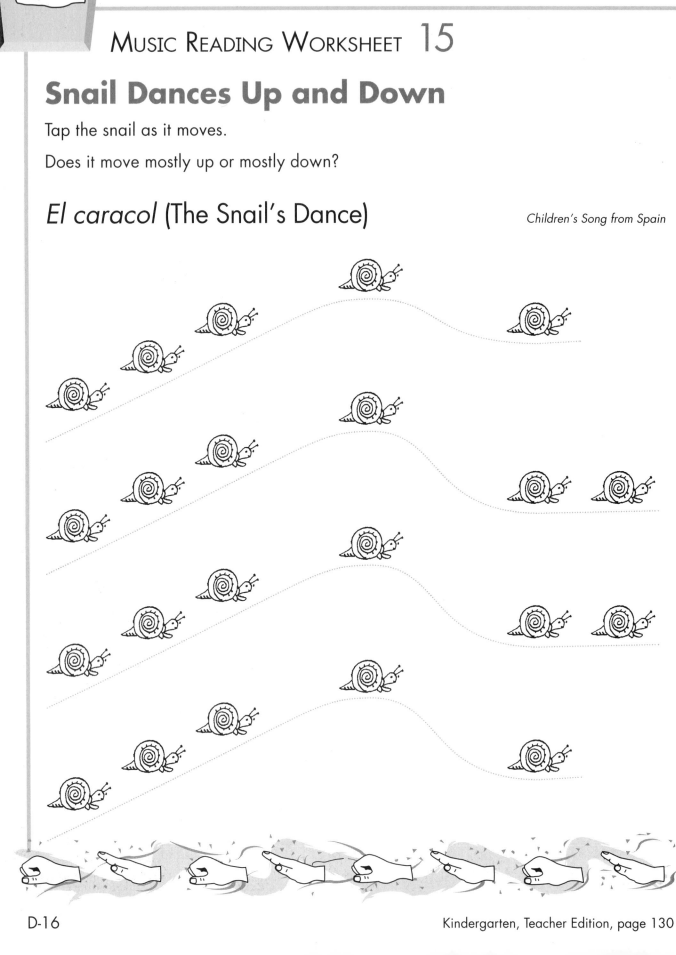

MUSIC READING WORKSHEET 16

Doggie Moves Up and Down

Tap the pawprints with the music.

Which part of the song moves up?

Ee jer ha ba go (The Hungry Dog)

Children's Song from China

MUSIC READING WORKSHEET 17

On a Log, One Frog, Two Frogs

Tap the frogs with the music.

On a Log, Mister Frog

Traditional Children's Song of the United States

MUSIC READING WORKSHEET 18

How Many Snails on a Beat?

Tap the snails with the music.

Find each empty leaf.

Will you draw one snail or two snails?

Bereleh (Little Snail)

Children's Song from Israel
Collected in Jerusalem by Rita Klinger

MUSIC READING WORKSHEET 19

A Lullaby with Parts

Tap the pictures on the beat.

Which parts of the song are the same?

Fais dodo (Close Your Eyes)

Folk Song from France

MUSIC READING WORKSHEET 20

Curwen Hand Signs

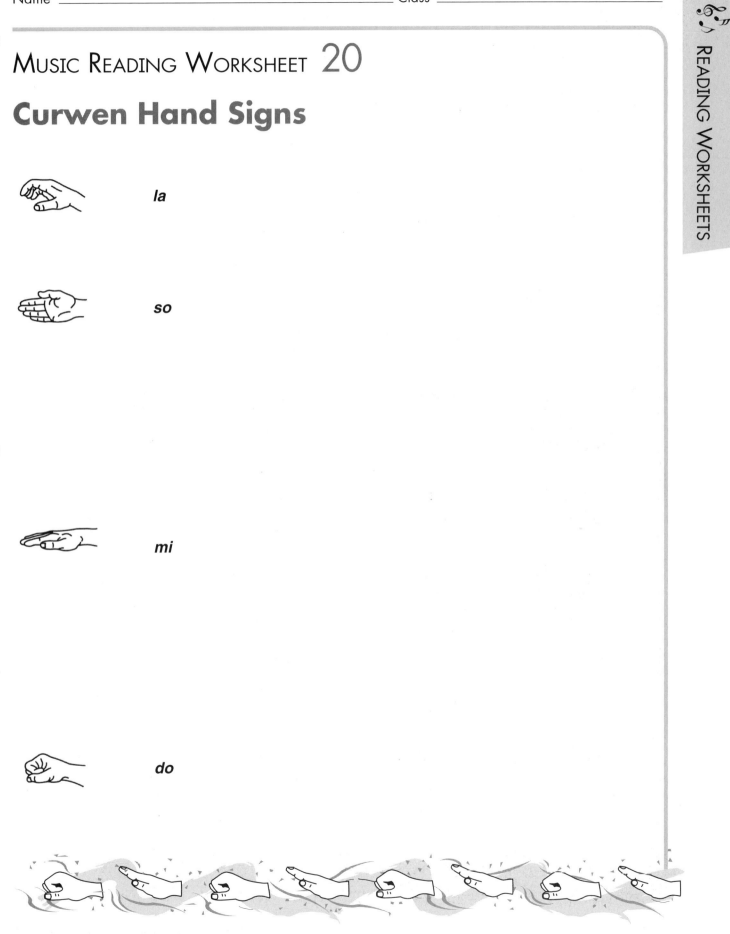

la

so

mi

do

Teacher Notes

ORFF

The Orff-process strategies in this section enrich the corresponding Teacher's Edition lesson plans with in-depth, developmentally-appropriate activities.

Table of Contents

ORFF 1

Movement/Reaction Training

Seasons

Words and Music by Jeanine Tesori

Help the children respond to verbal cues. For example, they might:

• Point an elbow toward the door.

• Shake hands with someone they don't know well.

• Touch someone who is wearing the color blue.

• Touch the floor with their wrists.

Next, try some verbal cues related to the song "Seasons" such as:

• Fall down to the ground like a falling leaf.

• Move like the cold winter wind.

• Move like a spring flower opening its petals.

• Melt in the hot summer sun.

Then, try some verbal cues that involve using loud and soft dynamics such as:

• Tiptoe across the room.

• Touch a wall with just one finger.

• Stamp their feet.

• Jump up and down.

Use either loud or soft dynamics for each verbal cue and have the children move gently or energetically as appropriate.

ORFF 1 (CONTINUED)

On another day, choose some instrumental sounds as cues for movement. For example, tell the children that when they hear

• a woodblock,	raise an arm.
• it again,	lower your arm.
• the cymbal,	turn in a circle.
• it again,	stop.
• the drum,	collapse.
• a glissando on a glock,	lift up their bodies.
• the gong,	stretch.
• the maracas,	shake.

Invite the children to suggest movements for other sounds. As a separate exercise, ask the children to use smaller or larger movements to suggest the loudness or softness of the sound.

ORFF

ORFF 2

Steady Beat

Hi-Dee-Roon

Traditional Calypso Song from Jamaica, Adapted

Set up barred instruments in *do*-pentatonic on D (D, E, F♯, A, and B). Use glocks, SX, AX, SM, and AM as available.

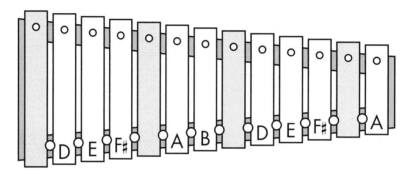

Have the children stand in a circle formation around the instruments. Have the children echo-say the following speech pattern on the steady beat:

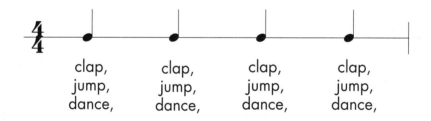

Choose a child to be the leader and stand in the center of the circle. As the leader claps on the call, the others either echo-say the speech pattern or imitate the movement on the response.

Then, repeat with *jump* and *dance*. Show the children how to play the speech pattern on any two bars of an instrument, resulting in tone clusters. Then invite some children to play tone clusters on the barred instruments during the response. Remind them to hold the mallets as if they are holding the handlebars of a tricycle.

ORFF **3**

Higher and Lower

I'm Tall, I'm Small

Traditional Children's Song

Place a soprano xylophone (SX) and a bass xylophone (BX) in the center of the room. Set up the instruments in *do*-pentatonic on Bb, leaving on the Bb, C, D, F and G bars.

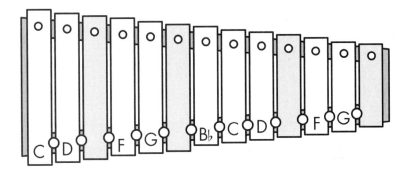

Improvise on the SX and the BX. As they listen, help the children notice the difference in size between the two, and then discover that the SX is higher in pitch than the BX.

As you improvise again, have the children:

- SX—Perform high movements; for example, they might walk on tiptoes, raise hands high up in the air.

- BX—Perform low movements; for example, touch the ground, crawl, or crouch down low.

Now switch back and forth between the two instruments and have the children move high or low as appropriate. Let the children see you play so that they can see high and low, as well as hear it and feel it.

When they are ready, have children face the other direction or move the instruments to a hidden location. Encourage them to perform either high or low movements, responding only to your aural cues. Use this movement activity as a B section to the song, which is the A section.

ORFF 4

Steady Beat

Jim Along, Josie

Folk Song from Oklahoma

Have the children stand in a circle around the barred instruments, which are set up in *do*-pentatonic on D (D, E, F♯, A, and B). Use glocks, SX, AX, SM, and AM as available.

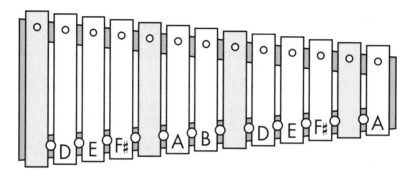

Choose a child to be the leader. As the leader walks around the inside of the circle, the others pat in time to his or her beat.

Repeat this activity with other children, who lead the class in performing the movements mentioned in the song—walk, hop, run, jump, tiptoe, crawl, swing, and roll.

Transfer to the barred instruments. Choose some children to play tone clusters on any two bars of an instrument in time to the leader's beat. Check to see that the children have a mallet in each hand, that they are playing in the center of the bars, and are letting the mallets bounce off the bars.

Orff 5

Echo

Who Has the Penny?

*Words and Music by Angela Diller
and Kate Stearns Page*

Have the barred instruments set up in *do*-pentatonic on D (D, E, F♯, A, and B). Use glocks, SX, AX, SM, and AM as available.

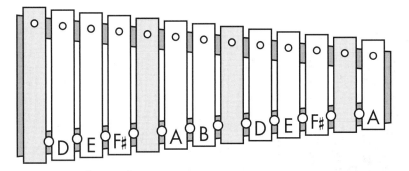

Say the following pattern from the song:

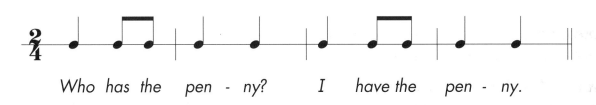

Who has the pen - ny?   I   have the pen - ny.

Invite the children to create other patterns as follows: Who has the _____, I have the _____. Then help them echo-pat the patterns with body percussion and later by playing tone clusters on pitched percussion.

Point out that in "Who Has the Penny?," one person echoes the entire group. As the children say or pat the rhythm of the chorus part, the soloists echo the rhythm on a barred instrument, using both hands.

ORFF

ORFF 6

High and Low

The Kangaroo Song

Words and Music by Peter Canwell

Have the instruments set up in *do*-pentatonic on F (F, G, A, C, D). Use SX as available and the BX.

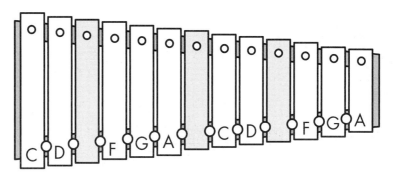

Say the refrain and have the children pat the beat.

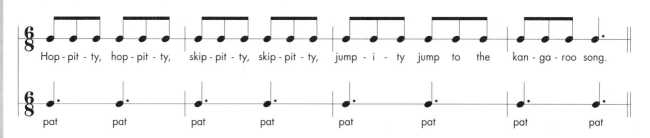

Hop - pit - ty, hop - pit - ty, skip - pit - ty, skip - pit - ty, jump - i - ty jump to the kan - ga - roo song.

pat   pat   pat   pat   pat   pat   pat   pat

As you play tone clusters on the SX to the beat, encourage the children to say the refrain and jump, standing high. Then, play the tone clusters on the BX and have them jump, crouching low. Alternate back and forth and have the children respond with the appropriate level of movement.

When they are ready, have the children face the other direction, or place the instruments in a hidden location. Encourage them to perform high or low movements, responding only to your aural cue.

Invite volunteers to play the SX part.

© PEARSON EDUCATION, INC.

● ORFF 7

Simple Accompaniment

Andy Pandy

Traditional

Set up the instruments in *do*-pentatonic on D (D, E, F♯, A, B). To ensure success, remove all bars except the D and A needed for the bordun.

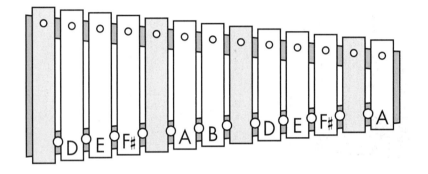

● **Speech Pattern:** "An-dy Pan-dy fine and dan-dy"

Body Percussion: Pat with both hands.

Instruments: Play a steady beat bordun on the AX.

Now play the bordun on AM. This will give the children a chance to compare the sound of the wood and metal instruments. Play the accompaniment with the song.

ORFF 8

Fast and Slow

Locomoto-vation

Words and Music by Bryan Louiselle

Have the instruments set up in *do*-pentatonic on F (F, G, A, C, D). Use SX, AX, and glocks as available.

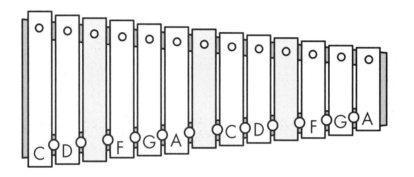

Improvise on the instruments as follows:

• At a fast tempo—have the children run or perform other fast movements.

• At a slow tempo—have the children walk or perform other slow movements.

• Alternate between fast and slow and have the children respond appropriately.

Invite the children to take turns improvising on the instruments while the others move in tempo with their playing.

After the performance, ask the player which tempo was intended and if the class responded appropriately. Then ask the class if the "player" did indeed play the tempo that he or she intended to play.

ORFF 9

High and Low Sounds

Here I Go!

Words by Amanda Green
Music by Ned Ginsburg

Have the instruments set up in *do*-pentatonic on C (C, D, E, G, A). Use SM or other high instruments as available and the BM or BX.

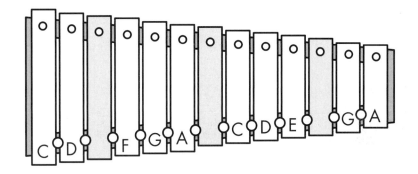

Review previous lessons on high and low sounds. Check that the children are aware that the soprano instruments sound higher than the bass instruments.

Review that the melody in each line of verse 1 moves from low to high, and in verse 2, from high to low. Then invite the children to add body percussion on the rests (3rd beat in measures 2, 4, 6, and 8).

Help the children transfer the body percussion to tone clusters on the barred instruments. Ask, "Which instruments should play on verse 1? Which should play on verse 2?" (Verse 1—SM, or higher instruments; verse 2—BM, or lower instruments.)

ORFF 10

Upward Sounds

Mary Wore Her Red Dress

Folk Song of the United States

Have the instruments set up in *do*-pentatonic on F (F, G, A, C, D). Use SX and AX as available.

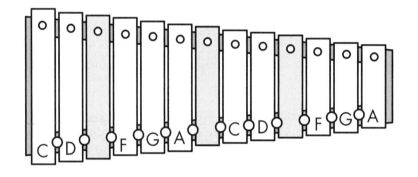

Play the first two measures of the song on the AX:

As you play this and other patterns, encourage the children to show their contours by moving a hand upward.

Demonstrate that 'upward' on the barred instruments means movement to the right.

Have the children practice patting ascending melody patterns on their desks or on the floor, moving their hands to the right. Invite volunteers to take turns playing ascending patterns on the barred instruments while the others show their contours with movement.

ORFF **11**

Downward Sounds

Busy Buzzy Bee

*Traditional Children's Song
of the United States*

Have the instruments set up in *do*-pentatonic on C (C, D, E, G, A). Use SX and AX as available.

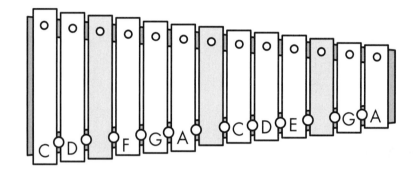

Play the first two-measure pattern on the AX:

As you play this and other descending melody patterns, encourage the children to show their contours by moving a hand downward.

Demonstrate that 'downward' on the barred instruments means movement to the left.

Have the children practice patting descending melody patterns on their desks or on the floor, moving their hands to the left. Invite volunteers to take turns playing descending melody patterns on the barred instruments while the others show their contours with movement.

Orff 12

Simple Bordun Accompaniment

Busy Buzzy Bee

Traditional Children's Song of the United States

Set up the instruments in *do*-pentatonic on C (C, D, E, G, A). To ensure success, remove all bars except the C and G needed for the bordun.

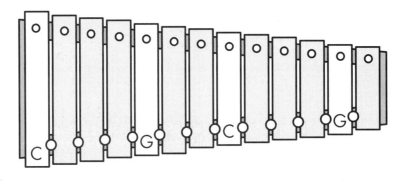

Speech Pattern: *Bu-sy, Buz-zy, Bu-sy, Buz-zy* (twice)

Body Percussion: Pat with both hands.

Instruments: Transfer the body percussion to the barred instruments and combine with the song.

● ORFF 13

Getting Faster/Getting Slower

Get on Board

African American Spiritual

Set up the instruments in *do*-pentatonic on F (F, G, A, C, D). Use SX and AX as available.

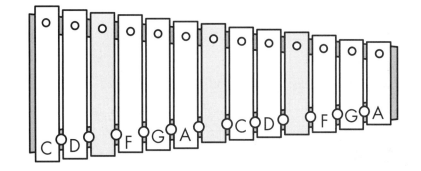

● Help the children form a circle. Invite volunteers to go into the center of the circle and form a "train" that is stopped at the station. Place the barred instruments off to the side.

As the "train" pulls out of the station slowly and gets gradually faster, the others pat to the "train's" beat.

Invite volunteers to accompany the train's movement by playing tone clusters on the barred instruments.

To show the train slowing down as it pulls into the station, help the children move quickly and then gradually slow down.

Orff 14

Simple Bordun Accompaniment

Little Spider

New English Words by Jean Sinor
Hungarian Folk Melody: "Csiga biga"

Set up the instruments in *do*-pentatonic on F (F, G, A, C, D). To ensure success, remove all bars except the F and C needed for the bordun.

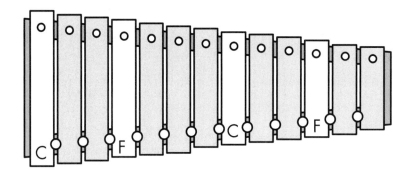

Speech Pattern: *Lit-tle spi-der, lit-tle spi-der*

Body Percussion: Pat with both hands.

Instruments: Transfer to the barred instruments and combine with the song.

● ORFF 15

Small Classroom Percussion

Mi cuerpo hace música

English Words by David Eddleman
Folk Song from Puerto Rico

Guide the children in exploring how various small percussion instruments produce sound by using a variety of appropriate ways to play each instrument.

Give the children a signal that tells them when to start and stop playing. Use louder sounds, such as chords on a piano or a large gong. Let the children play their instruments and respond to the signal as you give it.

As the children try out various instruments, lead them to understand that we can group instruments into families based on the action needed to produce the various sounds; for example, by shaking, scraping, or striking the instruments. Some possibilities are:

● • Shake—jingle bells, maracas

● • Scrape—guiro, sand blocks

• Strike—drums, tone blocks, triangle

Invite the children to volunteer playing their instruments for the class. Encourage the others to describe the sounds that they hear. You might let them take turns hiding in a corner of your classroom while they guess the name of the instrument being played and how it was played.

When they are ready, help the children place the instruments in groups according to their material composition. A diagram is provided below.

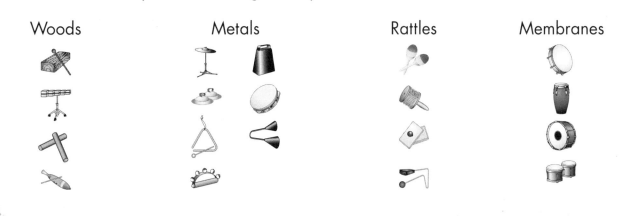

| Woods | Metals | Rattles | Membranes |

ORFF 16

Small Classroom Percussion

Jamaican Folk Melody
New Words and Music Adaptation by
Massie Patterson and Sammy Heyward

Bam, chi, chi, bam

Have the children echo the following rhythm:

As you play the recording, help the children discover that this pattern occurs in the refrain of "Bam, chi, chi, bam."

Ask, "How many times do you hear this pattern?" (Three)

Lead the children as they:

• Say the rhythm pattern and add body percussion.

• Play the pattern on your small classroom percussion instruments.

• Play the pattern in groups—woods, metals, rattles, and membranes.

• Discover that the refrain has four phrases and that there are four groups (families) of small classroom percussion.

• Practice playing the rhythm pattern.

• Decide on an order in which each group will accompany one phrase of the refrain.

• Use the pattern as an introduction and/or coda to the song.

ORFF 17

Long Sounds and Short Sounds

Old Blue

Mountain Song of the Southern United States

Have the instruments set up in *do*-pentatonic on F (F, G, A, C, D). Use SX, AX, SM, AM, SG, AG as available. Group together all xylophones, metallophones, and glockenspiels.

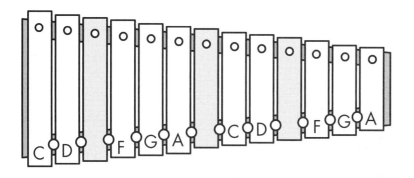

Improvise on a metallophone, spacing your sounds well apart. Encourage the children to:

- Perform either long or short movements to match the sounds that you play.

- Continue their movements as long as they hear the sound.

- Discover that the metallophone produces longer sounds.

Repeat with the glockenspiel and then with the xylophone.

Guide the children to discover that the xylophone produces shorter sounds.

Have three children go to the instruments: one to a xylophone, one to a metallophone and one to a glockenspiel. At your cue, each child improvises on his or her instrument as the others perform long or short movements as appropriate.

ORFF 18

Timbre of the Instrumentarium

Rhymes

Set up the instruments in *do*-pentatonic on C, removing the Fs and Bs.

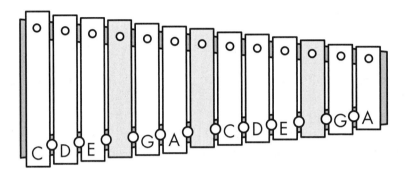

Group together similar instruments (woods and metals), families of instruments (xylophones, metalophones, and glocks), and similar voiced instruments (bass, alto, soprano):

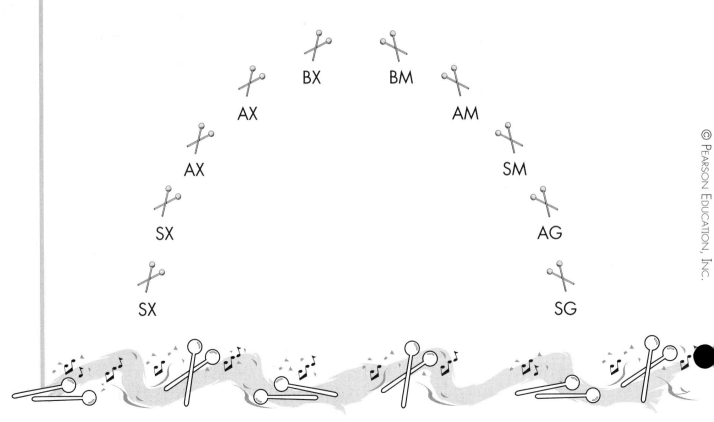

© PEARSON EDUCATION, INC.

ORFF 18 (CONTINUED)

Let the children play each instrument, experimenting with the different sounds it can produce. Encourage the children to watch you (the conductor) and not to look at their instruments.

Extend one palm up and out and hold a mallet in the other hand. Ask the children to watch the mallet in your hand.

- When your mallet is in the air, the children's mallets are in the air.

- When you lower the mallet to touch the palm of your other hand, the children lower their mallets and play their instruments.

Next, place two rings or carpet squares in the center of the floor. Explain that one ring represents the xylophones (woods) and the other ring represents the metallophones and glockenspiels (metals).

- When you step inside the woods ring—xylophones play.

- When you step inside metals ring—metallophones and glockenspiels play.

- Explore the different timbre of the woods and metals.

When the children are ready, place three rings in the center—xylophones, metallophones, and glockenspiels. Encourage children to play as you step in and out of each ring. Then, invite volunteers to take turns being "the conductor."

Invite children to improvise an accompaniment for the rhymes on pp. 136–137.

ORFF

Orff **19**

Simple Bordun Accompaniment

Oliver Twist

Traditional Folk Song of the British Isles and the United States

Set up the instruments in *do*-pentatonic on D (D, E, F♯, A, B). To ensure success, remove all bars except the D and A needed for the bordun.

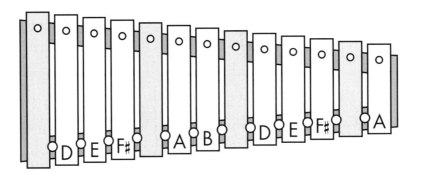

Speech Pattern: *Head, nose, knees, toes* (twice)

Body Percussion: Pat the body parts listed above.

Instruments: Transfer to the barred instruments and combine with the song.

ORFF 20

Play the Beat, Play the Rhythm

Oliver Twist

Traditional Folk Song of the British Isles and the United States

Set up the instruments in *do*-pentatonic on D (D, E, F♯, A, and B.) Use glockenspiels, SX, AX, and SM as available.

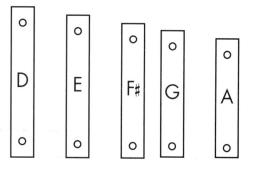

When the instruments are ready, place them in a circle large enough to accommodate the entire class.

Lead the children in clapping the "heart beat," or the steady beat, of "Oliver Twist," and then the "humpty dumpty kind of beat," or its rhythm.

Now have the children take a place along the edge of the circle. As they sing the song, help the children respond as follows:

• Perform the movements mentioned in the song.

• Walk to the right on the words *around you go* in the last line.

When the song comes to an end, let those children who are by instruments accompany their classmates' reprise of the song by playing either the steady beat or the word rhythms. You might add a bordun on the bass xylophone to make the accompaniment more interesting.

Repeat this activity numerous times to give as many children as possible an opportunity to play the Orff instruments.

ORFF 21

Getting Louder/Getting Softer

Storm Dance

Words and Music by Rick Bassett

Set up the instruments in *do*-pentatonic on C (C, D, E, G, A). Use SX, AX, SM, AM, SG, and AG as available.

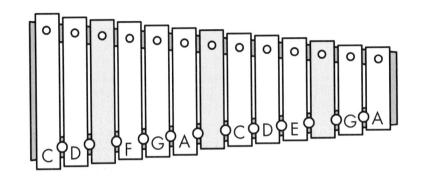

Have the children echo the following speech pattern:

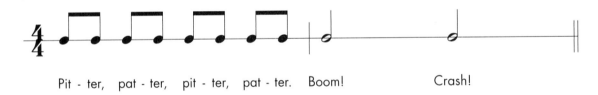

Pit - ter, pat - ter, pit - ter, pat - ter. Boom! Crash!

Help the children discover that this pattern can be found in the speech piece. Ask, "How many times do you hear this pattern?" (Four times)

Say the rhythm pattern. As the children pat the pattern, encourage them to alternate hands on the eighth notes (beginning with the left hand), and then pat with both hands together on the half notes *Boom!* and *Crash!*.

Kindergarten, Teacher Edition, page 145

ORFF 21 (CONTINUED)

Transfer to the barred instruments.

Encourage the children to play the eighth notes softly and get louder and then play the tone clusters *forte*.

Help the children discover that we can make music get louder by having one instrument play gradually louder or by adding more instruments to the ensemble.

Explore with the children the many ways to use dynamics as they create their storm with the barred instruments.

ORFF

ORFF 22

Simple Bordun Accompaniment

On a Log, Mister Frog

Traditional Children's Song of the United States

Set up the instruments in *do*-pentatonic on D (D, E, F♯, A, B). To ensure success, remove all bars except the D and A needed for the bordun on the xylophones.

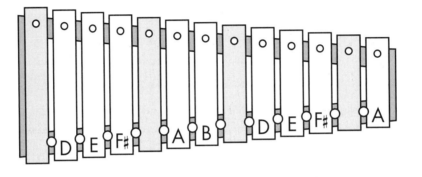

Speech Pattern: Recite this pattern: "Sit and sing from night to day-break"

Body Percussion: Pat with both hands.

Instruments:

• Measures 1–4: Play the bordun on the AX and SX, as available.

• Measures 5–6: Play tone clusters on the glocks and metallophones, as available, or choose any other vocal or instrumental sound.

© Pearson Education, Inc.

● ORFF 23

Simple Bordun Accompaniment

Roll Over

Folk Song from the United States

Set up the instruments in *do*-pentatonic on F (F, G, A, C, D). To ensure success, remove all bars except the F and C needed for the bordun.

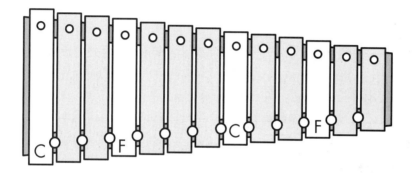

Speech Pattern: "I need more room"

Body Percussion: Pat with both hands.

Instruments: Play the pattern on the AX and SX and then on the AM and SM. This will give them a chance to compare the sound of the woods with the metals.

If you play the song at a slower tempo, a quarter note pattern may be easier for the children to play.

© PEARSON EDUCATION, INC.

ORFF **24**

Simple Bordun Accompaniment

Circle Round the Zero

African American Game Song

Set up the instruments in *do*-pentatonic on D (D, E, F#, A, B). To ensure success, remove all bars except the D and A needed for the bordun.

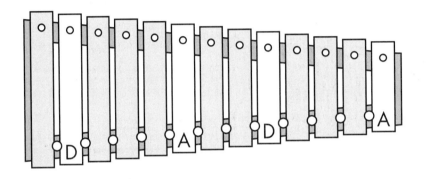

Speech Pattern: Recite the following pattern twice:

Round the ze-ro

Body Percussion: Pat with both hands.

Instruments: Play on the AX and SX as available and combine with the song.

● ORFF 25

INSTRUMENTARIUM

Abbreviations of Instruments on a Score

Winds

SoR	Sopranino Recorder
SR	Soprano Recorder
AR	Alto Recorder
TR	Tenor Recorder
BR	Bass Recorder

Mallet Instruments

SG	Soprano Glockenspiel
AG	Alto Glockenspiel
SX	Soprano Xylophone
AX	Alto Xylophone
BX	Bass Xylophone
CBX	Contrabass Xylophone
SM	Soprano Metallophone
AM	Alto Metallophone
BM	Bass Metallophone

Percussion—Metals

Tr	Triangle
FC	Finger Cymbals
JB	Jingle Bells
BT	Bell Tree
AB	Agogo Bells
CB	Cow Bell
Cym	Cymbals
W	Slide Whistle

Percussion—Woods

WB	Wood Block
ToB	Tone Block
C	Castanets

Sh	Shakers
M	Maracas
Cb	Cabasa
R	Ratchet
Rt	Rattles
TeB	Temple Blocks
VS	Vibra Slap
Cl	Claves
Gu	Guiro
LD	Log Drum
SB	Sand Blocks
Af	Afuchi

Percussion—Membranes or Skins

HD	Hand Drum
Tam	Tambourine
BD	Bongo Drums
CD	Conga Drum
SD	Snare Drum

Large Percussion

HC	Hanging Cymbal
G	Gong
BD	Bass Drum

Tuned Instruments

G	Guitar
P	Piano
Tp	Timpani
DB	Double Bass

ORFF

Teacher Notes

SIGNING

Table of Contents

SIGNING

SIGNING 1

*Children's Rope Skipping Song
from the Sendai District, Japan
English Words Courtesy of
the CP Language Institute, New York*

Kuma san (Little Bear)

short	bear	short	bear
Little	Bear,	Little	Bear,

turn

Turn   yourself around.

short	bear	short	bear
Little	Bear,	Little	Bear,

please   **gesture: touch the ground**

Now please touch the ground.

Signing 1 (CONTINUED)

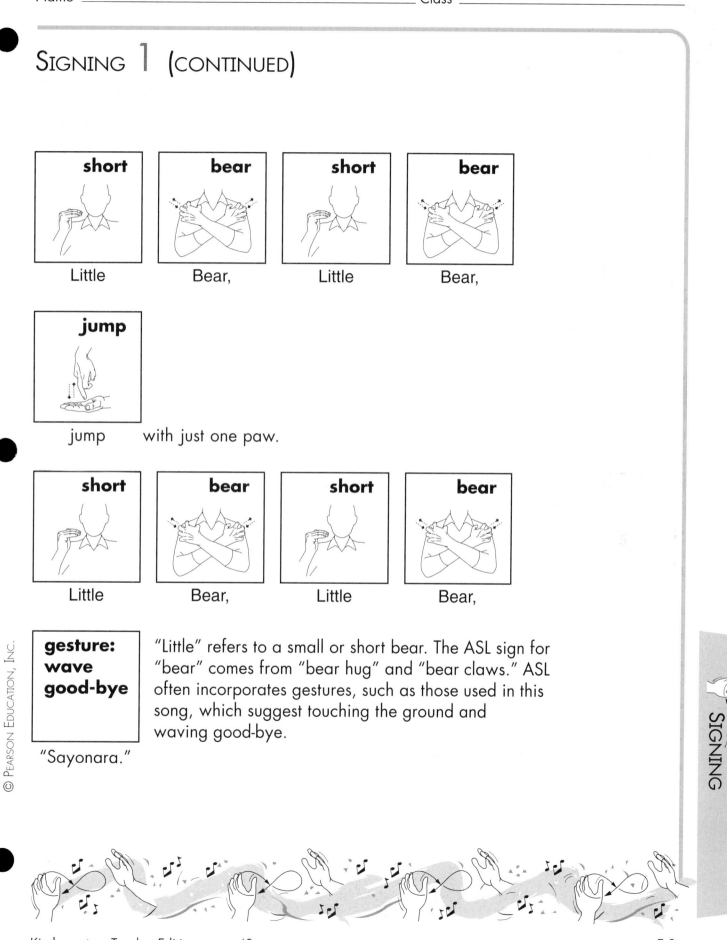

short | **bear** | **short** | **bear**

Little | Bear, | Little | Bear,

jump

jump   with just one paw.

short | **bear** | **short** | **bear**

Little | Bear, | Little | Bear,

**gesture:
wave
good-bye**

"Little" refers to a small or short bear. The ASL sign for "bear" comes from "bear hug" and "bear claws." ASL often incorporates gestures, such as those used in this song, which suggest touching the ground and waving good-bye.

"Sayonara."

SIGNING

SIGNING 2

Ég a gyertya (Candle Burning Bright)

Children's Song from Hungary
English Words by Rochelle Mann

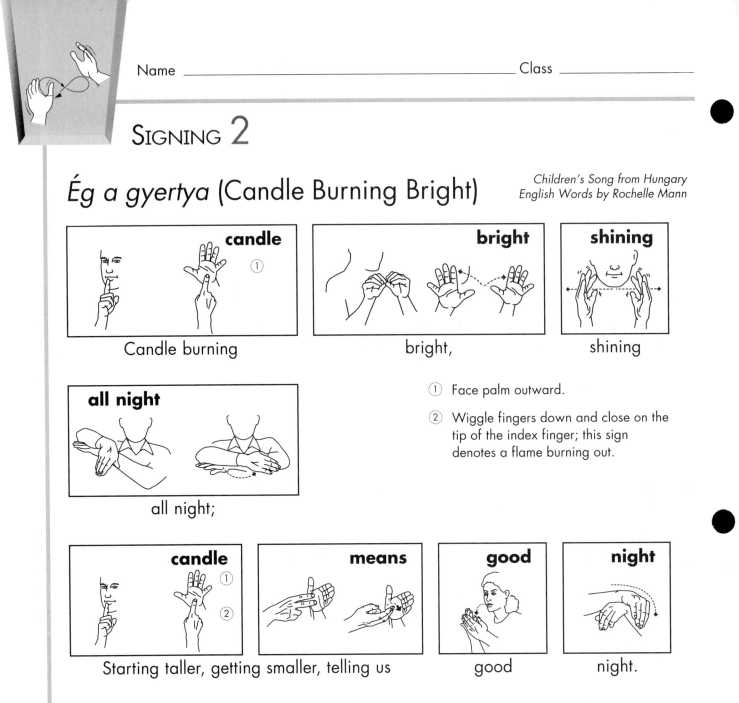

candle ①
Candle burning

bright
bright,

shining
shining

① Face palm outward.

② Wiggle fingers down and close on the tip of the index finger; this sign denotes a flame burning out.

all night
all night;

candle ① ②
Starting taller, getting smaller, telling us

means

good
good

night
night.

For the sign "candle," the index finger represents the candle and the wiggling fingers represent the flame.

The sign for the lyrics *starting taller, getting smaller* is a good example of the way American Sign Language communicates. The sign "paints" a picture of the candle burning out. Signs do not translate words, but rather, the meanings of them.

The sign for *all night* represents the sun's movement beneath the horizon.

Signing 3

Yang wa wa (Nursery Song)

Children's Song from Taiwan
English Words by William Shao

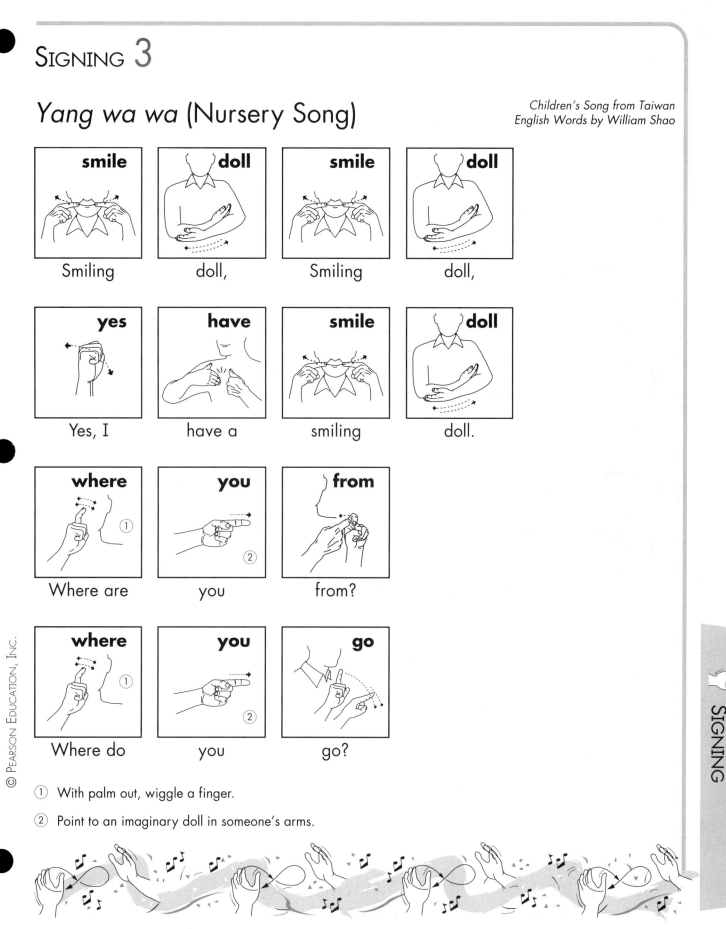

smile — Smiling	**doll** — doll,	**smile** — Smiling	**doll** — doll,
yes — Yes, I	**have** — have a	**smile** — smiling	**doll** — doll.

where ① — Where are	**you** ② — you	**from** — from?
where ① — Where do	**you** ② — you	**go** — go?

① With palm out, wiggle a finger.

② Point to an imaginary doll in someone's arms.

SIGNING

SIGNING 3 (CONTINUED)

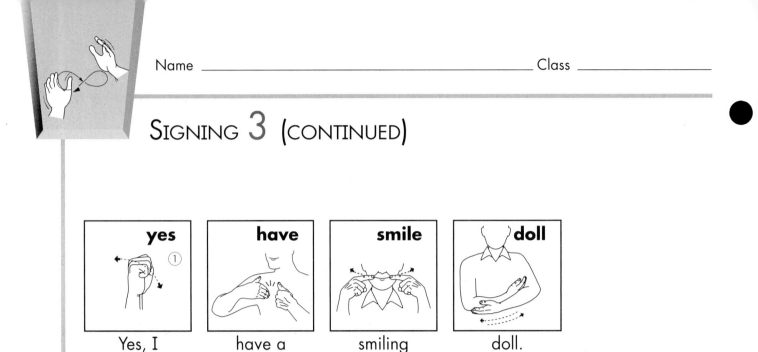

yes	have	smile	doll
Yes, I	have a	smiling	doll.

For the sign "yes," the fist represents the head nodding up and down. ASL does not use helping verbs, such as "are," or articles, such as "a." Also, ASL does not usually include pronouns such as "I."

① Face the palm outward.

SIGNING 4

Sharing

Words and Music by Marcy Marxer

① Point the finger outward.

SIGNING 4 (CONTINUED)

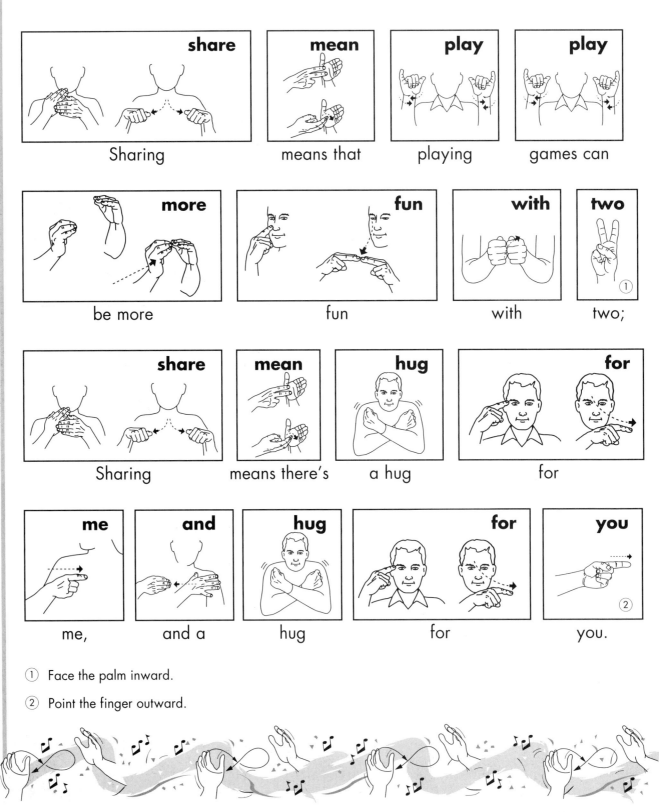

share — Sharing

mean — means that

play — playing

play — games can

more — be more

fun — fun

with — with

two — two; ①

share — Sharing

mean — means there's

hug — a hug

for — for

me — me,

and — and a

hug — hug

for — for

you — you. ②

① Face the palm inward.

② Point the finger outward.

SIGNING 5

Farmer in the Dell

Old Singing Game

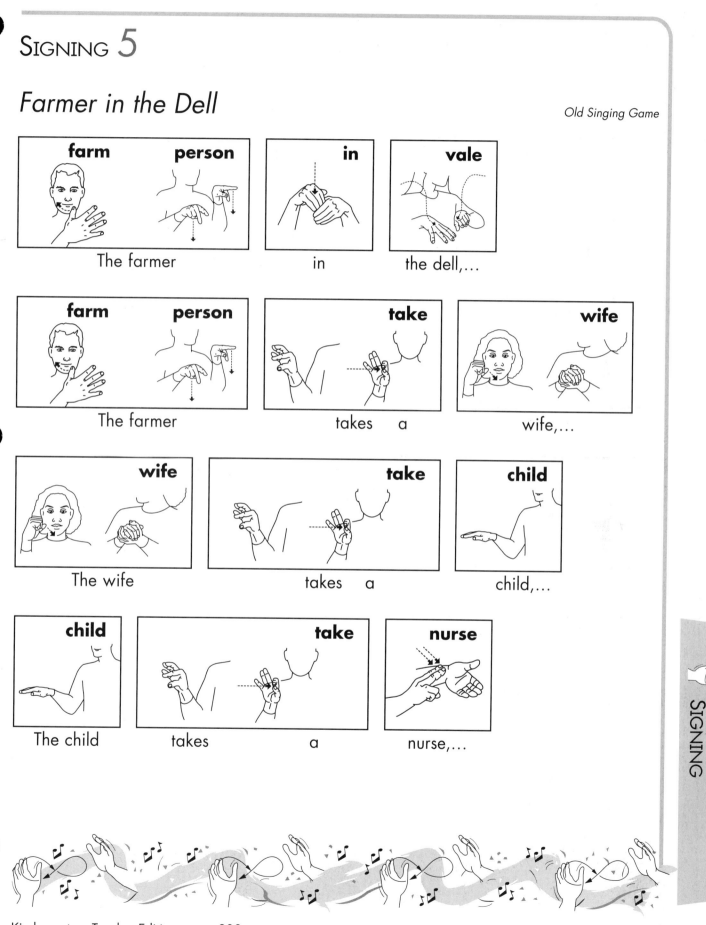

farm **person**	**in** **vale**
The farmer	in the dell,...

farm **person**	**take**	**wife**
The farmer	takes a	wife,...

wife	**take**	**child**
The wife	takes a	child,...

child	**take**	**nurse**
The child	takes a	nurse,...

SIGNING

SIGNING 5 (CONTINUED)

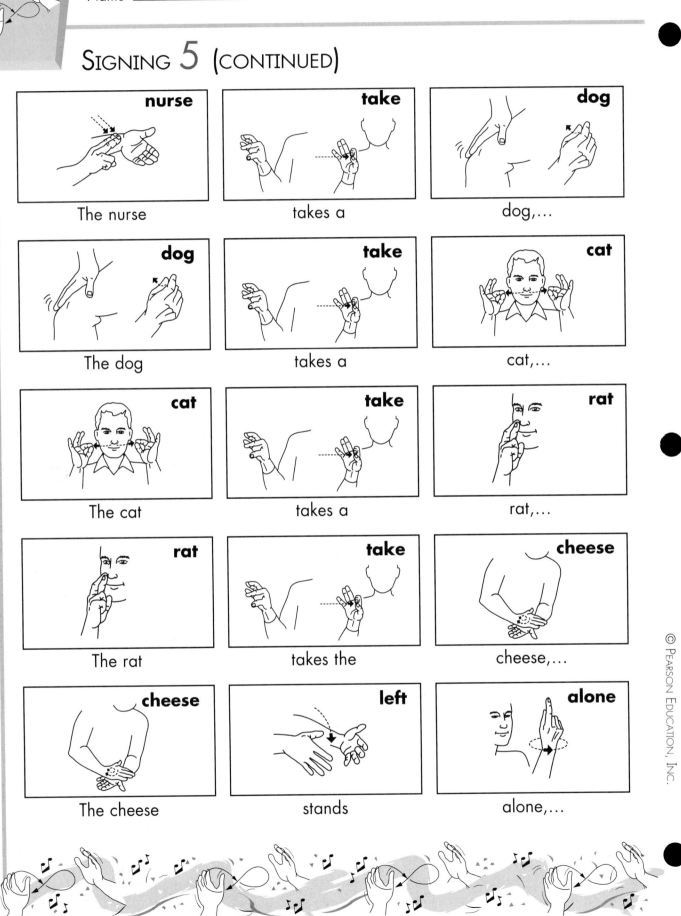

| nurse | take | dog |
| The nurse | takes a | dog,... |

| dog | take | cat |
| The dog | takes a | cat,... |

| cat | take | rat |
| The cat | takes a | rat,... |

| rat | take | cheese |
| The rat | takes the | cheese,... |

| cheese | left | alone |
| The cheese | stands | alone,... |

Kindergarten, Teacher Edition, page 232

SIGNING 6

My Valentine

Words by Frank Hagerman
Music by Ruth Stevens Porter

you	**my**	**valentine**	**valentine**	**valentine**
①	②			
Will you	be my	valentine,	valentine,	valentine?

you	**my**	**valentine,**	**I love you**
①	②		
Will you	be my	valentine?	I love you.

yes (gesture: nod head)	**I**	**your**	**valentine**	**valentine**	**valentine**
		③			
Yes,	I'll be	your	valentine,	valentine,	valentine.

yes (gesture: nod head)	**I**	**your**	**valentine**	**I love you**
		③		
Yes,	I'll be	your	valentine.	I love you.

① Point the finger outward or towards a specific person.

② Place the palm flat against your chest.

③ Face the palm outward or towards a specific person.

SIGNING

Signing 6 (continued)

Questions that require a "yes" or "no" answer are indicated by raising one's eyebrows, as if anticipating a response.

The sign for "I love you" is becoming well-known even among hearing people. It is often used as a farewell sign when leaving a loved one.

The sign for "yes" is a fist nodding up and down, but simply nodding the head while signing the words *I'll be your valentine* also means "Yes, I'll be your valentine."

"My Valentine" may be signed by partners, with Signer 1 asking the question and Signer 2 responding.

SIGNING

Manual Alphabet

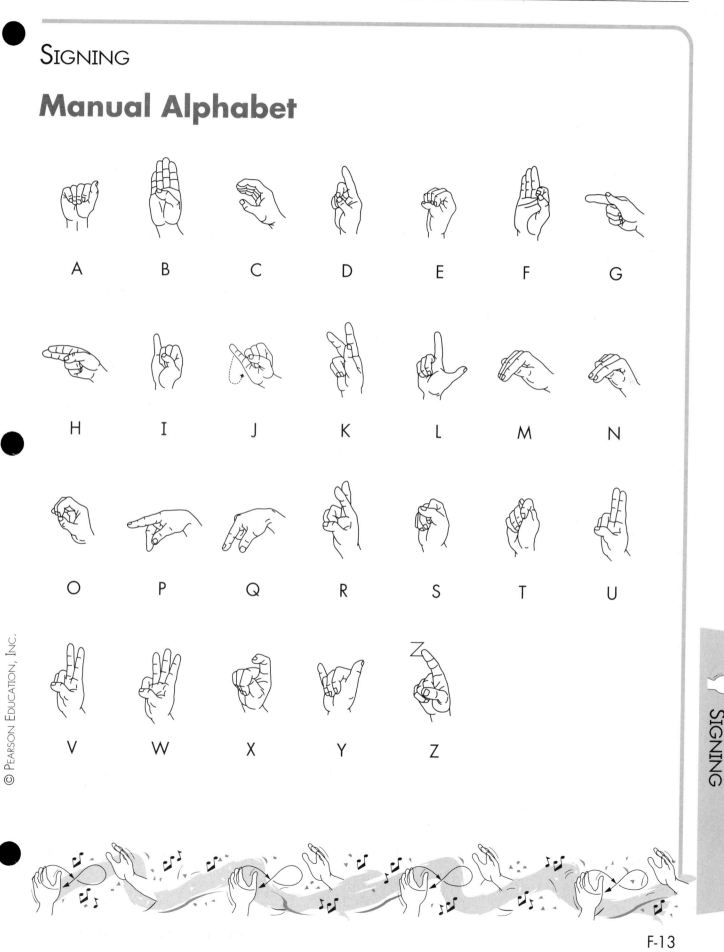

SIGNING

Signing

Numbers

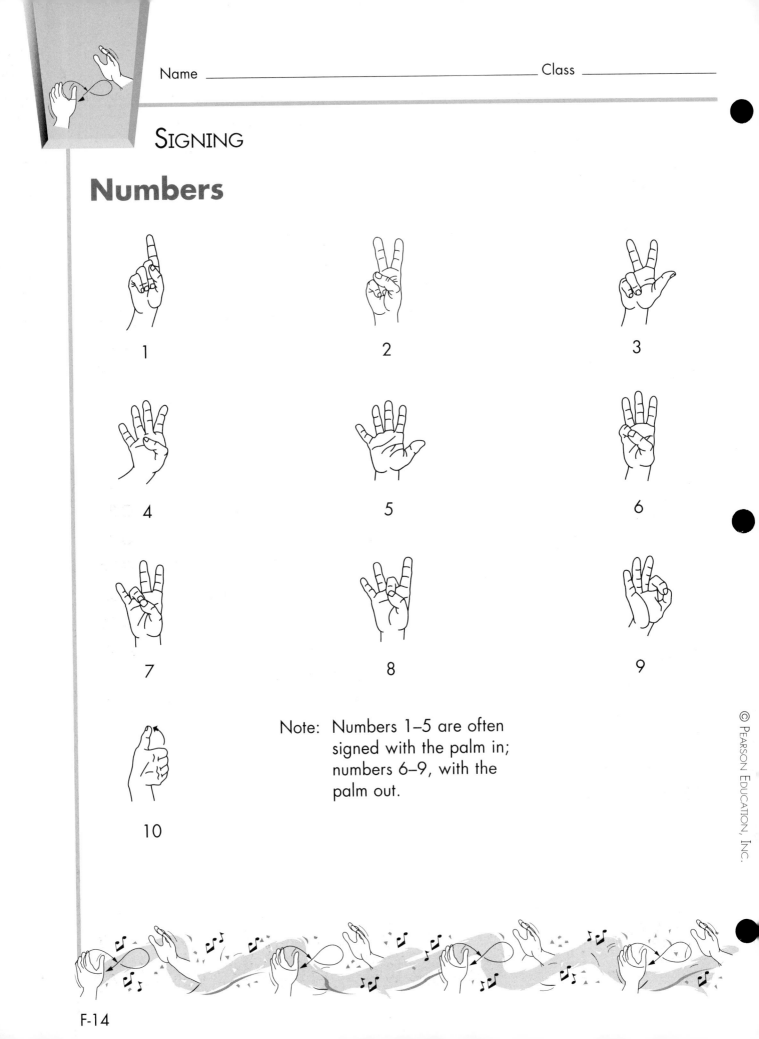

1

2

3

4

5

6

7

8

9

10

Note: Numbers 1–5 are often signed with the palm in; numbers 6–9, with the palm out.

ACTIVITY MASTERS
Table of Contents

Text has been provided on each page so that you may explain to the children what they are to do.

ACTIVITY MASTER 1

A Letter to Home

This year, your child will be participating in a music class designed to foster lifelong appreciation of music through active music making. The sequenced music instruction will help your child develop musical skills and understanding, using music of various styles from the United States and around the world. In addition to developing specific musical skills, your child's studies in other areas will be enhanced by instruction that links concepts across the curriculum.

Your child will also have opportunities to participate in theme-based music making. Some possible themes include American music, world music, friends, families, self-esteem, animals, ecology, storytelling, choral singing, seasons, and celebrations. Your child may also be involved in classroom and/or school-wide performances, and you will be invited to attend or volunteer to assist with these performances.

You can also reinforce your child's music learning at home. Consider listening to music together and talking about it. Ask your child to share songs learned in music class. Attend local concerts to help foster appropriate audience behavior. These experiences will help make music meaningful at school, at home, and in the community.

Sincerely,

ACTIVITIES

ACTIVITY MASTER 2

Una Carta al Hogar

Este año, su niño(a) tomará parte en una clase de música que le ayudará a adquirir una apreciación de música durante toda la vida mediante su participación en actividades musicales. La instrucción de música, que está estructurada en una secuencia lógica, le ayudará a su niño(a) a desarrollar destrezas y conocimientos musicales, al experimentar distintos estilos de música de los Estados Unidos y de todas partes del mundo. Además del desarrollo de destrezas musicales, su niño(a) mejorará en los otros campos de estudio porque la instrucción relaciona conceptos provenientes de todo el plan de estudios.

Su niño(a) también tendrá oportunidades de tomar parte en actividades musicales basadas en un tema. Entre estos temas hay música americana, música mundial, amigos, familias, auto-estima, animales, ecología, cuentos, canto coral, estaciones y celebraciones. Tal vez su niño(a) pueda estar envuelto en actuaciones en la clase y/o para toda la escuela, y se le invitará a usted(es) a asistir o a ayudar con estas actuaciones como voluntario(a). Usted(es) también puede(n) reforzar en casa el aprendizaje de música de su niño(a). Consideren escuchar a música juntos y después hablar sobre lo que oyeron. Pídale a su niño(a) que comparta con usted(es) las canciones que ha aprendido en la clase de música. Llévelo(la) a conciertos de la zona para ayudarle a experimentar en la audiencia conducta apropriada. Todo esto ayudará a hacer que la música sea una experiencia significativa para su niño(a) en la escuela, en casa y en la comunidad.

Sinceramente,

ACTIVITY MASTER 3

Loud and Soft Around Me

Draw a circle around the loud sounds.

● ACTIVITY MASTER 4

Sounds Like Three Little Pigs!

Cut out the animals and the word strips. Now use these pieces to tell the story of "Three Little Pigs." Paste the animals on a sheet of paper. Place each word strip high or low on the paper to show what type of sound the animal makes.

Oink, oink, oink　　　　**Wee-wee-wee**

ACTIVITY MASTER 5

Sing, Speak, Shout, Whisper

Match each voice to the correct picture.

ACTIVITIES

ACTIVITY MASTER 6

Animals Make Loud and Soft Sounds

Make each animal sound. Put an X next to the soft sounds. Then color the pictures.

ACTIVITY MASTER 7

Our Loud and Soft Moves

What are each of these people doing? Does the movement make a loud sound? Draw an X next to the loud sounds.

● ACTIVITY MASTER 8

All Johnny's Moves

Johnny Mister Brown knows lots of ways to move. Use the pictures to follow what he does as you listen to verses 2–6 of "Johnny Mister Brown." Then show how Johnny moves in each verse. Cut out the pictures. Put them in order on a sheet of paper and paste them down.

One hand up   **One hand down**

| **One hand up** | **One hand down** | **Stamp your feet.** |
| **Walk with me.** | **Run along.** | **Turn around.** |

ACTIVITY MASTER 9

Beat—No Beat

Most music has a steady beat. Some sounds have no beat. Which sounds have a steady beat? Mark these sounds with an X.

ACTIVITY MASTER 10

Playing Along with the Three Bears

Play different keys on a keyboard. Draw a line from the low sounds to Papa Bear. Draw a line from the medium sounds to Mama Bear. Draw a line from the high sounds to Baby Bear. Now tell the story of Goldilocks and the Three Bears, using low, medium, and high sounds on the keyboards. What sounds—high, medium, or low—will you use for Goldilock's voice?

ACTIVITY MASTER 11

Voice Sounds High and Low

Make these sounds with your voice.
Put an X next to the low sounds.

● **ACTIVITY MASTER** 12

My High and Low Pictures

Imagine something or someone making a high sound.
Draw a picture of a high sound.
Then draw a picture of a low sound.

HIGH SOUND

LOW SOUND

Activity Master 13

Counting on the Beat

2, 4, 6, 8

Traditional Children's Rhyme

Say these numbers: 2, 4, 6, 8.
Tap the pictures as I say the rhyme.

Write the numbers to finish the speech piece.

_____ _____ _____ _____

© Pearson Education, Inc.

ACTIVITY MASTER 14

Moving Upward or Downward

Circle the people or things that move upward.

ACTIVITY MASTER 15

Rain Music

Circle instruments in Row 1 that will make a soft rain sound. Then circle instruments in Row 2 that will make a loud rain sound. Play your instruments to create a rainstorm. Follow the picture at the bottom of the page.

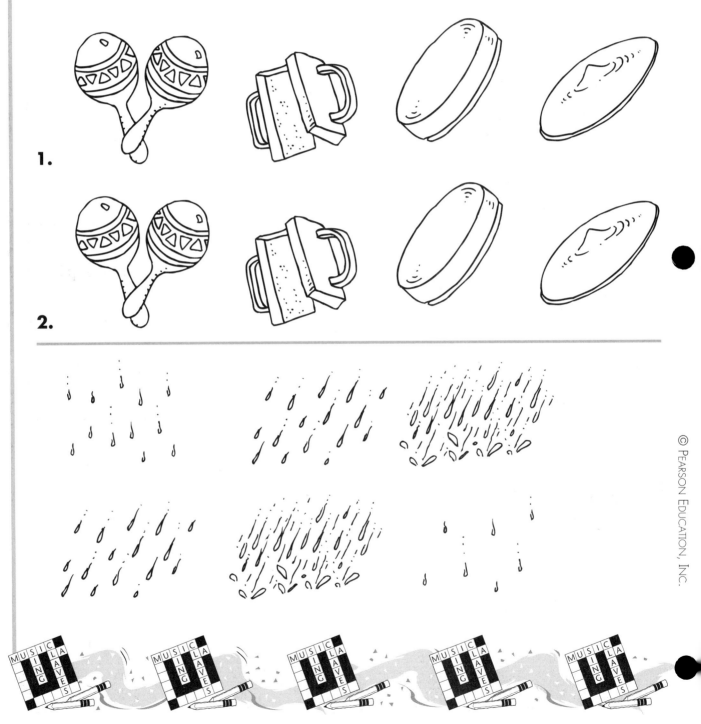

1.

2.

Kindergarten, Teacher Edition, page 81

ACTIVITY MASTER 16

The Band on the Bus

Work with a partner to cut out these pictures and words. Put the pictures in the order that they are mentioned in the song. Match the action words to the pictures. Then choose an instrument for each sound maker on the bus.

people	money	up and down
		round and round
wheels	wipers	"Beep, beep, beep!"
		"Clink, clink, clink!"
horn	driver	"Swish, swish, swish!"
		"Move on back!"

ACTIVITY MASTER 17

Playing Under Moonlight

Say the rhyme and tap the rhythm. Choose an instrument to play for each part of the speech piece. Play only when I point to your row of pictures. Let's take turns playing these parts as an introduction to "Moon, Moonlight."

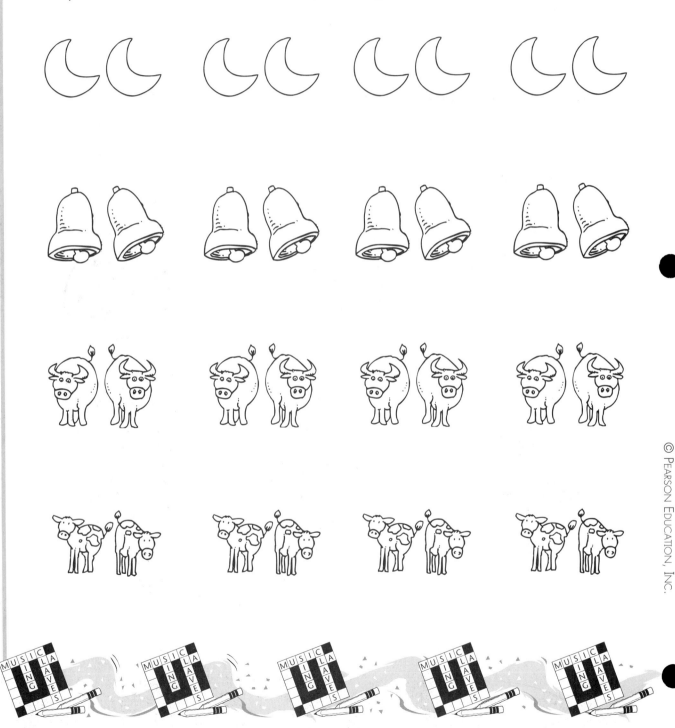

Kindergarten, Teacher Edition, page 90

ACTIVITIES

ACTIVITY MASTER 18

If You're Happy, Show It!

Find the pictures of ways to show you are happy. Help us create new words about them for "If You're Happy." Later, we'll create words and movements about other feelings.

If you're happy and you know it . . .

ACTIVITY MASTER 19

A Circle Song with Parts

What do the children do in each verse?
Put the pictures in the correct order.

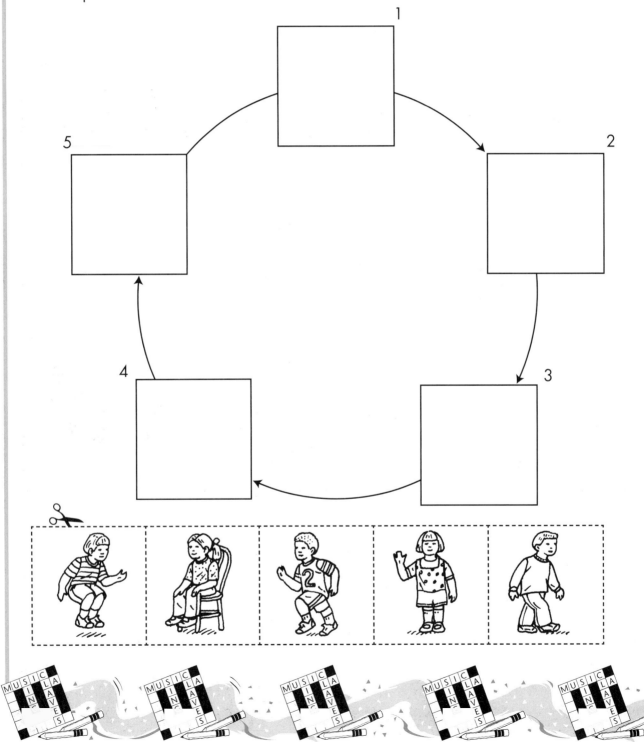

Kindergarten, Teacher Edition, page 125

ACTIVITY MASTER 20

Nanny Goat's Repeated Pattern

Tap the goats to follow the pitches of Nanny Goat's repeated pattern. Then cut out the melody pattern cards. Arrange the cards to show the order in which you hear the melody patterns.

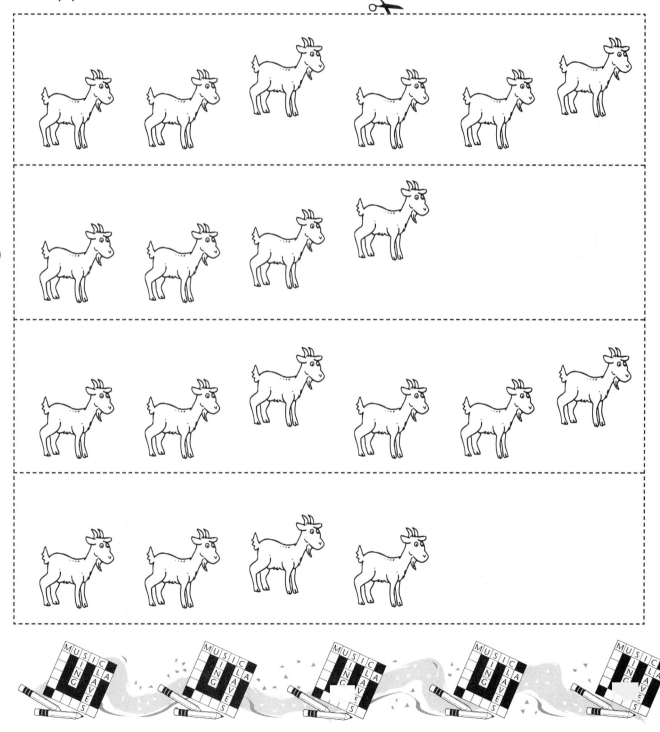

ACTIVITY MASTER 21

My Sound Painting

Color these shapes and cut them out. Glue the shapes in the box below, using the order that you like best. Help us create sounds for each shape. Run your finger along the shapes as the class plays your sound painting.

ACTIVITY MASTER 22

Painting with Words and Sounds

You can be an artist, too! Listen for the art words in "Painting Song" that tell what helps to make a painting special. Use the pictures and labels to help you follow along. Then create your own painting, using some or all of the details mentioned in the song. Create sounds for your painting.

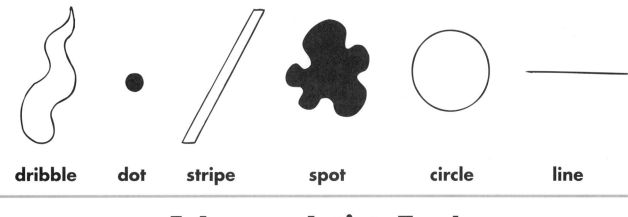

| **dribble** | **dot** | **stripe** | **spot** | **circle** | **line** |

I Am an Artist, Too!

ACTIVITY MASTER 23

The Frog's Merry Song

Cut out one of the frogs and glue it to a craft stick. As you sing "The Frog Song" with the recording, listen for the words *Can you hear this merry song?* Make your puppet jump from one lily pad to the other. On what lily pad will we start to sing this pattern?

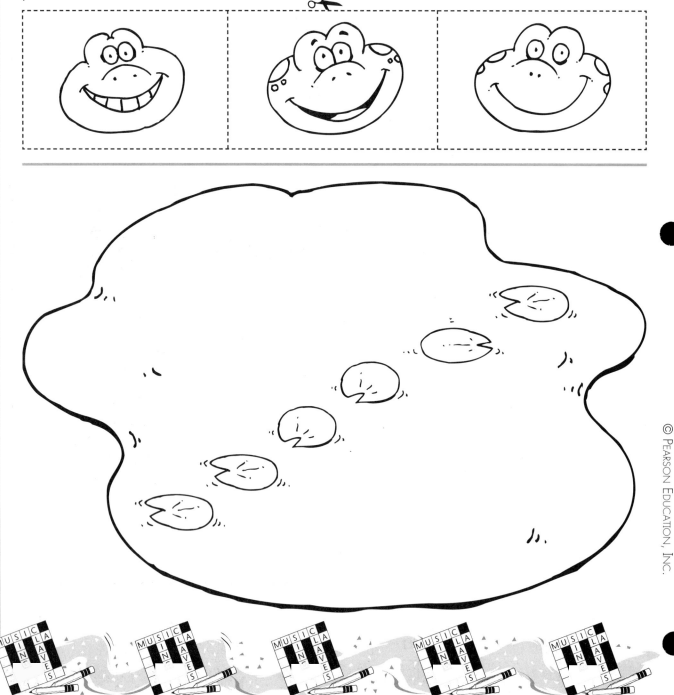

ACTIVITY MASTER 24

Frolicking Frogs

Frogs can be alike and different, too. They can move in different ways. Look at where each frog is. What kinds of movements will it do? Color the frogs and create movements. Perform your movements for a favorite frog for the class.

ACTIVITY MASTER 25

Picnic Patterns

Work with a partner to cut out these pictures. Find which things don't belong on a picnic. Then sort the picnic foods to show the order in which they are mentioned in "Going on a Picnic." As you sing the song again, hold up the card when the picnic food is named. On another day, let's create a rhythm chain or new words for the song about the other things on the page.

ACTIVITY MASTER 26

First I... Then I...

Use the pictures to help you remember how to move to "Number One, Touch Your Tongue." Tap each picture on the steady beat as we say the speech piece. Then write the numbers 1–10 at the bottom of the page. Create other words that rhyme with each number.

1

2

3

4

5

6

7

8

9

10 **Do it all again.**

ACTIVITY MASTER 27

Looby Loo Left and Right

Following directions can help you have fun as you singing games. Use these pictures to help you practice moving left and right with "Looby Loo."

LEFT　　　　　　　　　　　　　　　　　　　　　　　　**RIGHT**

Kindergarten, Teacher Edition, page 210

ACTIVITY MASTER 28

A Story of Six Little Ducks

What happens in each picture?
Tell the story of the song.
Use numbers to put these pictures in order.

ACTIVITY MASTER 29

A Story in Sound

Pretend to go on a country walk.
Circle the things that make sounds.
What things do not make sounds?

Kindergarten, Teacher Edition, page 235

Name ______________________ Class ____________

ACTIVITIES

ACTIVITY MASTER 30

Circus Sights and Sounds

1. Create an accompaniment for this poem.

2. Which instruments will you choose?

3. Show the mood of the poem as you play.

The Circus

by Jane Beethoven

If I were in the circus
I'd balance on my toes,
And tame a lion and ride a horse
While standing on my nose.

I'd be a very funny clown
I'd climb up high and tumble down.
The crowd would cheer and yell out, "WOW."
And upside down,
I'd take a bow.

ACTIVITY MASTER 31

Music for a Bear Hunt

Choose some words from the poem.
What will you use to accompany them?
Draw a line to the instruments you will use.

On a lovely day in the month of May,

I walked along

Singing a song.

I saw a bear,

And his cub in a lair;

And then ran away,

For what could I say

To a bear and a cub in a lair?

ACTIVITIES

ACTIVITY MASTER 32

Bear Beat, Bear Rhythms

As you listen to "Two Bears," tap the grass patches. Then tap the bears. Play a sound on the drum for each bear. Then draw your own pattern of bears, using the grass patches at the bottom of the page. Play this rhythm pattern with the song.

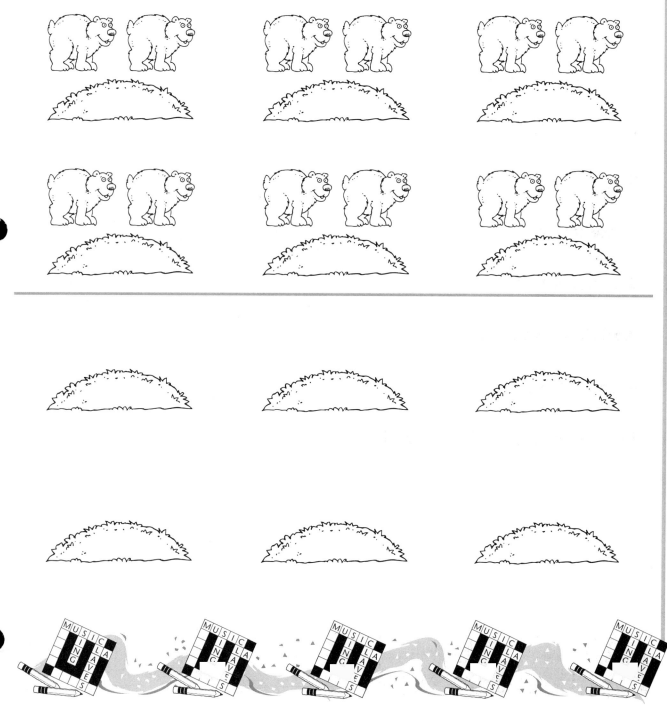

© PEARSON EDUCATION, INC.

ACTIVITY MASTER 33

Up-and-Down Merry-Go-Round

Which words from the song move downward?
Draw an X next to these parts.
Which words go with these parts?

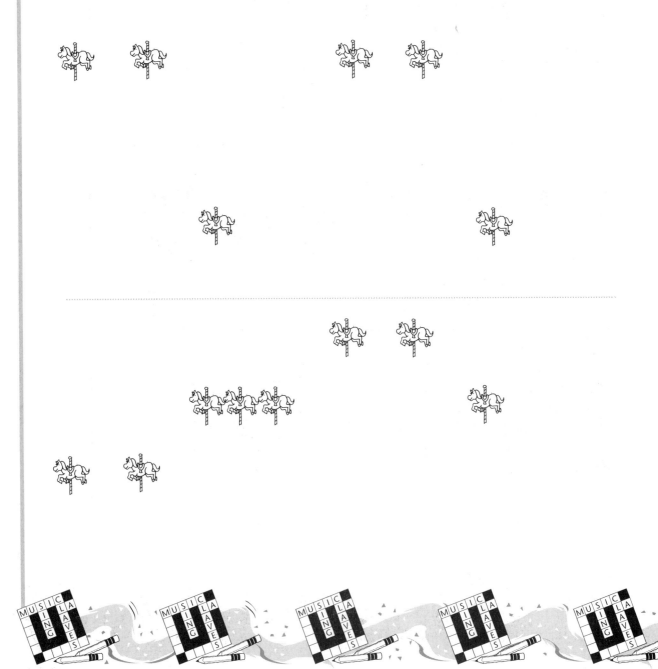

ACTIVITY MASTER 34

When the Piano Plays Along

Which performers are being accompanied by a piano?
Put an X next to these people.

ACTIVITY MASTER 35

Instrument Parts

Each instrument is missing one of its parts.
Draw a line from the instrument to the missing part.

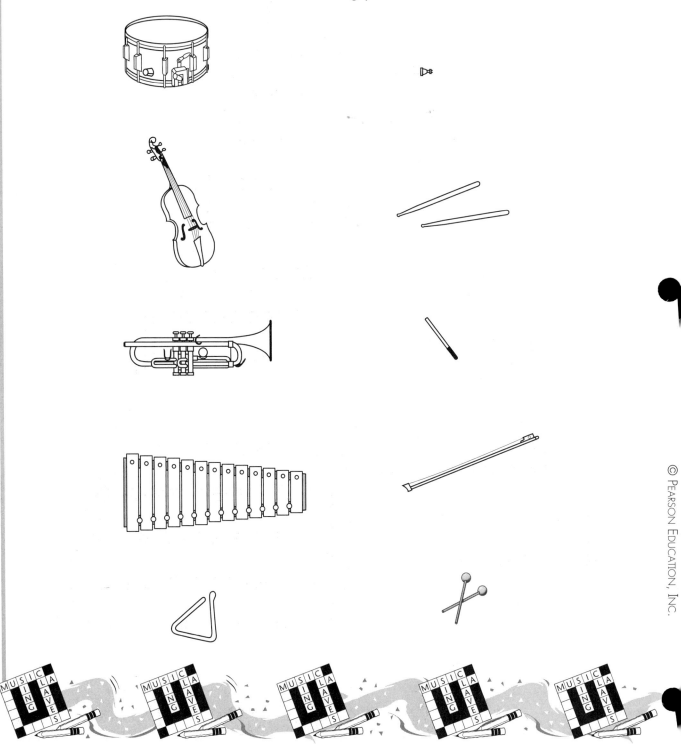

● ACTIVITY MASTER 36

Bell Diagram

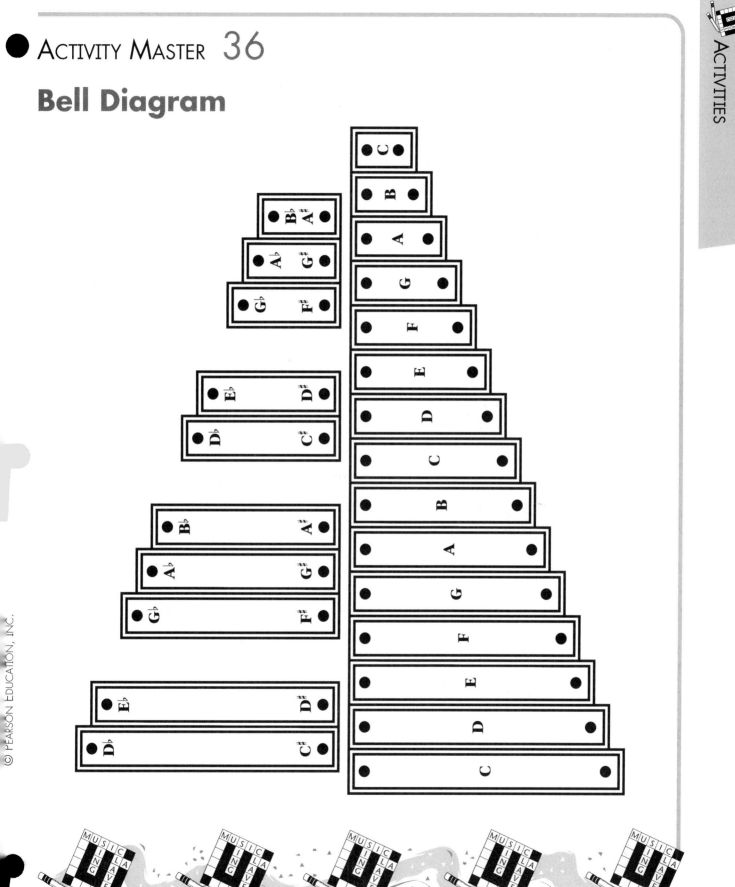

ACTIVITY MASTERS ANSWER KEY

G-4   **Activity Master 3: Loud and Soft Around Me**

The loud sounds are: the wrecking ball (row 1); the train whistle (row 2); and the drill (row 3).

G-5   **Activity Master 4: Sounds Like Three Little Pigs!**

During Verse 1, the three little pigs sing with very high voices. During verse 2, the three little pigs might sing with voices that are lower than those they used for Verse 1. The mother sings in a high or a medium high voice throughout the song.

G-6   **Activity Master 5: Sing, Speak, Shout, Whisper**

The following voices in Column 1 match:
1. singing: Picture 3
2. speaking: Picture 4
3. shouting: Picture 2
4. whispering: Picture 1

G-7   **Activity Master 6: Animals Make Loud and Soft Sounds**

The soft sounds are that of the: chickadee (Row 2) and possibly the bee (Row 2).

G-8   **Activity Master 7: Our Loud and Soft Moves**

The movements shown are: a man tapping his foot (loud or soft), a ballerina twirling on point (soft); a boy mowing the lawn (loud); and a man honking his horn (loud).

● ACTIVITY MASTERS ANSWER KEY (CONTINUED)

G-9   Activity Master 8: All Johnny's Moves

The movements mentioned in "Johnny Mister Brown" are as follows:
Verse 1: 'round and 'round (twice)
Verse 2: One hand up; one hand down
Verse 3: Stamp your feet (twice)
Verse 4: Walk with me (twice)
Verse 5: Run along (twice)
Verse 6: Turn around (twice)

G-10   Activity Master 9: Beat — No Beat

The sounds represented, which have a steady beat, are those of: the tick tock of the grandfather clock, the children marching, the siren, and the children jumping rope.

G-11   Activity Master 10: Playing Along with the Three Bears

The voices that suit each character in "Goldilocks and the Three Bears" are: Papa Bear (low), Mama Bear (medium), Baby Bear (very high), and Goldilocks (less high that Baby Bear's voice).

G-12   Activity Master 11: Voice Sounds High and Low

The low sounds shown are those of the: bear and tugboat in Row 1.

G-14   Activity Master 13: Counting on the Beat

The numbers that finish the speech piece are: *2, 4, 6, 8.*

G-15   Activity Master 14: Moving Upward or Downward

The people or things that move upward are the: girl climbing the stairs (Row 1) and the plane ascending into the sky (Row 2).

G-18 **Activity Master 17: Playing Under Moonlight**

Possible instruments to use are: Row 1 (moon)—triangle; Row 2 (bells)—sleigh bells; Row 3 (bulls)—hand drum); Row 4 (calves)—tambourine.

G-19 **Activity Master 18: If You're Happy, Show It!**

The movements that might show happiness are: smiling, wiggling, and jumping.

G-20 **Activity Master 19: A Circle Song with Parts**

The pictures show 1: jump 2: rest 3. walk 4. run 5. say "Hi!"

G-26 **Activity Master 25: Picnic Patterns**

The picnic foods in "Going On a Picnic" are mentioned in this order: hot dogs, salad, ice cream, and melon.

G-29 **Activity Master 28: A Story of Six Little Ducks**

The pictures should be numbered as follows: Row 1—1 and 3; Row 2. The single duck is mentioned during Lines 3-5 of each verse.

G-30 **Activity Master 29: A Story in Sound**

The things that do not make sounds are the grass, flowers, rocks, and ladybug.

G-35 **Activity Master 34: When the Piano Plays Along**

The performers that are accompanied by a piano are shown in Picture 1 in Rows, 1, 2, and 3.

G-36 **Activity Master 35: Instrument Parts**

The instruments match with their parts as follows: drum—pair of sticks; violin—bow; trumpet; mouthpiece; xylophone; mallets; triangle; stick.

Teacher Notes

ART CREDITS

Assessment

B-2, Donna Catanese; B-3, Donna Catanese; B-4, George Hamblin; B-5, Donna Catanese; B-6, Burgandy Beam; B-7, Linda Howard Bittner; B-8, Linda Howard Bittner; B-9, Joe Rogers; B-10, George Hamblin; B-11, George Hamblin; B-12, Linda Howard Bittner; B-13, Joe Rogers; B-15, Donna Catanese; B-16, Donna Catanese, George Hamblin; B-16, Burgandy Beam; B-19, Linda Howard Bittner; B-20, George Hamblin; B-21, George Hamblin.

Reading

D-2, Bobbi Tull; D-3, Burgandy Beam; D-4, Bobbi Tull; D-5, Burgandy Beam; D-6, Burgandy Beam; D-7, Bobbi Tull; D-8, Bobbi Tull; D-9, Bobbi Tull; D-10, Burgandy Beam; D-11, Bobbi Tull; D-12, Burgandy Beam; D-13, Bobbi Tull; D-14, Burgandy Beam; D-15, Burgandy Beam; D-16, Bobbi Tull; D-17, Burgandy Beam; D-18, Bobbi Tull; D-19, Burgandy Beam; D-20, Bobbi Tull.

Orff icons

All art Tony Nuccio.

Signing

All art Burgandy Beam.

Activity Master

G-4, Dan Bridy; G-5, Mike Dammer; G-6, Linda Howard Bittner; G-7, Reggie Holladay; G-8, Reggie Holladay; G-9, Mike Dammer; G-10, Linda Howard Bittner; G-11, Mike Dammer; G-12, Reggie Holladay; G-14, Dan Bridy; G-15, Dan Bridy; G-16, Mike Dammer; G-17, Mike Dammer; G-18, Mike Dammer; G-19, Mike Dammer; G-20, Dan Bridy; G-21, Mike Dammer; G-22, Mike Dammer; G-23, Mike Dammer; G-24, Mike Dammer; G-25, Mike Dammer; G-26, Mike Dammer; G-27, Mike Dammer; G-28, Mike Dammer; G-29, Linda Howard Bittner; G-30, Linda Howard Bittner; G-32, Linda Howard Bittner; G-33, Mike Dammer; G-34, Reggie Holladay; G-35, Linda Howard Bittner; G-36, Burgandy Beam.

ACKNOWLEDGMENTS

Credits and appreciation are due publishers and copyright owners for use of the following:
A-2: "O ma washi" (Go Around the Cat's Eye) © 1995 Silver Burdett Ginn. **A-5:** "Mbombera" © 2002 Pearson Education, Inc. **A-6:** "Kuma san" (Little Bear) from *Favorite Songs of Japanese Children* by Hanako Fukuda. © Alfred Publishing Co., Inc. Used with permission of the publisher. **A-10:** "Mon son pha" (Mon Hides the Cloth) Rhythmic setting © 2002 Pearson Education, Inc. **A-13:** "Kunolounkwa," Oneida Lullaby adapted by Joanne Shenandoah. Reprinted by permission of Joanne Shenandoah. **A-18:** "Ee jer ha ba go" (The Hungry Dog) © 1998 Silver Burdett Ginn. **A-19:** "Bereleh" (Little Snail), from *Multicultural Perspectives in Music Education*, 2nd edition, edited by William M. Anderson and Patricia Shehan Campbell. Copyright © 1996 by Music Educators National Conference. Used with permission. **A-21:** "Fais dodo" (Close Your Eyes) © 1956 Silver Burdett Company. **A-26:** "¿Dónde lo escondí?" (Where Did I Hide It?) **A-29:** "Sh'ney dubim" (Two Bears) Words by Judith Eisenstein from Songs of Childhood, selected and edited by Judith Eisenstein and Frieda Prensky, 1955. Published by the United Synagogue Commission on Jewish Education. **A-32:** "Vamos a cantar" (Let's Sing), from *Diez Deditos* by José-Luis Orozco, copyright © 1997 by José-Luis Orozco, Used by permission of Dutton Children's Books, a division of Penguin Putnam Inc. and José-Luis Orozco. **A-36:** "Rinsho, rinsho" Japanese Folk Song. Translation © 1993 Gloria J. Kiester. Used by permission. **E-2:** "Seasons" Words and Music by Jeanine Tesori. © 2000 Jeanine Tesori. Used by permission. ORFF accompaniment by Pearson Education, Inc. **E-4:** "Hi-Dee-Roon" from The Collection of Massie Patterson and the Carib Singers. Used by permission of Samuel Patterson. ORFF accompaniment by Pearson Education, Inc. **E-7:** "Who Has The Penny?" (from A Pre-School Music Book). Words and music by Angela Diller and Kate Stearns Page. Copyright © 1936 (Renewed) by G. Schirmer, Inc. ORFF accompaniment by Pearson Education, Inc. **E-8:** "Kangaroo Song" by Peter Canwell. Copyright © 1975 by Peterman & Co. Ltd. Used by Permission. ORFF accompaniment by Pearson Education, Inc. **E-10:** "Locomoto-vation" Words and Music by Bryan Louiselle. © 2000 Bryan Louiselle and Frog Prince Music. ORFF accompaniment by Pearson Education, Inc. **E-11:** "Here I Go!" Music by Ned Ginsburg; words by Amanda Green. © 2000 Ned Ginsburg and Amanda Green. Used by permission. ORFF accompaniment by Pearson Education, Inc. **E-12:** "Mary Wore Her Red Dress" © 2002 Pearson Education, Inc. ORFF accompaniment © 2002 Pearson Education, Inc. **E-13; 14:** "Busy Buzzy Bee" Words and Music by Katinka S. Daniel, from Kodaly in Kindergarten. Copyright © 1981 by Fostco Music Press, a division of Shawnee Press, Inc. ORFF accompaniment by Pearson Education, Inc. **E-18:** "Bam, chi, chi, bam" (Based on a traditional song) TRO-© Copyright 1963 (Renewed) Ludlow Music, Inc. New York, NY. ORFF accompaniment by Pearson Education, Inc. **E-24:** "Storm Dance" Words and Music by Rick Bassett. © 2000 Rick Bassett. Used by permission. ORFF accompaniment by Pearson Education, Inc. **E-26:** "On a Log, Mister Frog" © 2002 Pearson Education, Inc. ORFF accompaniment © 2002 Pearson Education, Inc. **E-28:** "Circle 'Round the Zero" © 1975 MMB Music, Inc., Saint Louis. ORFF accompaniment © 2002 Pearson Education, Inc. **F-2:** "Kuma san" (Little Bear) from *Favorite Songs of Japanese Children* by Hanako Fukuda. © Alfred Publishing Co., Inc. Used with permission of the publisher. English version by Pearson Education, Inc. **4:** "Ég a gyertya" (Candle Burning Bright) English words © 2002 Pearson Education, Inc. **7:** "Sharing" Words and Music by Marcy Marxer © (p) Marcy Marxer, 2 Spoons Music, ASCAP. From Changing Channels on Rounder Records. **11:** "My Valentine", Words by Frank Hagerman from *The Magic of Music—Book One*, © 1970, 1965, by Ginn and Co. Music by Ruth Stephens Porter from The Kindergarten Book of Our Singing World series, © 1969, 1967, 1949 by Ginn and Co. Reprinted by permission of Pearson Education, Inc. **162:** "Yang wa wa" (Nursery Song) English words © 1988 Silver Burdett Ginn.

The editors of Scott Foresman have made every attempt to verify the source of "Los pollitos" **A-23**, "¿Dónde lo escondí?" **A-26**, and "Vamos a hacer la ronda" **A-32**, but were unable to do so. Every effort has been made to locate all copyright holders of material used in this book. If any errors or omissions have occurred, corrections will be made.